BASICS OF MANUFACTURING

Fundamental Concepts for Decision Makers

J. David Viale

A FIFTY-MINUTE™ SERIES BOOK

CRISP PUBLICATIONS, INC.
Menlo Park, California

BASICS OF MANUFACTURING

Fundamental Concepts for Decision Makers

J. David Viale

CREDITS
Managing Editor: **Kathleen Barcos**
Editor: **Follin Armfield**
Typesetting: **ExecuStaff**
Cover Design: **Carol Harris**
Artwork: **Ralph Mapson**

Printed in the United States of America by Bawden Printing Company.

English language Crisp books are distributed worldwide. Our major international distributors include:

CANADA: Reid Publishing Ltd., Box 69559—109 Thomas St., Oakville, Ontario, Canada L6J 7R4. TEL: (905) 842-4428, FAX: (905) 842-9327

Raincoast Books Distribution Ltd., 112 East 3rd Avenue, Vancouver, British Columbia, Canada V5T 1C8. TEL: (604) 873-6581, FAX: (604) 874-2711

AUSTRALIA: Career Builders, P.O. Box 1051, Springwood, Brisbane, Queensland, Australia 4127. TEL: 841-1061, FAX: 841-1580

NEW ZEALAND: Career Builders, P.O. Box 571, Manurewa, Auckland, New Zealand. TEL: 266-5276, FAX: 266-4152

JAPAN: Phoenix Associates Co., Mizuho Bldg. 2-12-2, Kami Osaki, Shinagawa-Ku, Tokyo 141, Japan. TEL: 3-443-7231, FAX: 3-443-7640

Selected Crisp titles are also available in other languages. Contact International Rights Manager Suzanne Kelly at (415) 323-6100 for more information.

Library of Congress Catalog Card Number 94-68195
Viale, J. David
Basics of Manufacturing
ISBN 1-56052-303-4

This book is printed on recyclable paper with soy ink.

ABOUT THIS BOOK

Basics of Manufacturing is not like most books. It stands out in an important way. It is not a book to read—it is a book to *use.* The "self-paced" format encourages readers to get involved and review new ideas immediately.

The approach of this book is to provide workers unfamiliar with manufacturing concepts and technology with a look at the broad categories of long-, medium-, and short-term planning as an integrated package. Specific topics including planning, forecasting, master scheduling, material planning, capacity planning and Just-in-Time manufacturing are covered, as well as basic manufacturing vocabulary.

Basics of Manufacturing can be used effectively in a number of ways. Here are some possibilities:

- **Individual Study.** Because the book is self-instructional, all that is needed is a quiet place, committed time and a pencil. By completing the activities and exercises, you receive both valuable feedback and action steps for improving your understanding of manufacturing basics.

- **Workshops and Seminars.** This book was developed from hundreds of interactive seminars and contains many exercises that work well with group participation. The book is also a refresher for future reference by workshop attendees.

- **Remote Location Training.** This book is an excellent self-study resource for managers, supervisors and managerial candidates not able to attend "home office" training sessions.

Even after this book has been used for training and applied in real situations, it will remain a valuable source of ideas.

TO THE READERS

Developing a cross-functional understanding will become a global competetive issue for "Information Age" workers.

As organizations continue to flatten and decision making is assumed by individuals and team-based groups, "cross-functional smartness" will play a vital competitive role.

Cross-functional smartness is defined as the ability to quickly grasp new information and data regarding different functional areas and use it effectively in decision-making situations.

The level of cross-functional smartness will be impacted primarily by how quickly you, your peers, suppliers and customers can acquire a basic understanding of other functional areas.

This book is intended to give you a fundamental understanding of one of the major functional areas—manufacturing.

With the mastery of this material, you will be well on your way to contributing to the globalization of basic manufacturing concepts.

J. David Viale

ABOUT THE AUTHOR

J. David Viale is the founder and president of the Center for Manufacturing Education, an international education and training company.

Dave's career in education started as a high school teacher, then he went on to teach at various colleges and universities.

His background includes management positions at Arthur Andersen, Hewlett-Packard, and Fairchild Semi Conductor. He was a practicing CPA and is certified in production and inventory management. (CPIM).

His diverse business and teaching background gives him a unique blend of theory, practicality and financial impact. With this diverse experience, he brings a cross-functional perspective to his classes, speeches, seminars and key executive presentations, which he delivers across the United States, Canada, Europe and the Far East.

He can be contacted at:

Phone: 408-973-0309
Fax: 408-973-1592

ACKNOWLEDGMENT

I wish to acknowledge Kathy Indermill, whose patience and teaching skills contributed to the written and instructional design of this book.

The graphics for the cover were produced by Daniel L. Burney, president of Ideas in Print.

Dedication—

This book is dedicated to my students. Thank you for the opportunity to do what I love—educate.

CONTENTS

CONTENTS (continued)

INTRODUCTION

The world of business is changing rapidly and dramatically. No longer will we see the stability of the past; reorganization is fast becoming standard. Business organizations are having to reinvent and reorganize themselves continuously in order to meet demands of the global marketplace.

The United States faces the challenge of developing the most highly educated and diverse workforce ever known. Because requirements for skill levels continue to increase, less-educated workers are struggling to find jobs. The competition for good jobs will only become more intense.

This book is for people entering the field of manufacturing and for those already employed in such functional areas as sales, marketing, finance, human resources, research and development (R&D), or any other support function, and who wish to develop a fundamental knowledge of how manufacturing works.

The information contained herein will be invaluable to your organization when customers ask your people to:

- Achieve faster turnaround times
- Carry their inventory at no charge.
- Be flexible, turn on a dime, and react to change with no increase in cost

More important, this book challenges you to upgrade your existing skills and acquire new ones. Regardless of your present skill level, you have the opportunity to increase your knowledge of manufacturing. Within these pages you will find:

- An organizing question at the beginning of each module to orient your thinking—all content that follows provides the answer to the question
- Learning objectives that aid in measuring and understanding
- The distilled essence of manufacturing theory and planning information
- Proven skill-building exercises for adding to your professionalism

INTRODUCTION (continued)

What's In It for You Personally?

No matter how process oriented your organization is, there is always room for improvement. By using the information and tools presented in this book, you will

- Acquire a fundamental understanding of various interrelations and responsibilities in the manufacturing environment
- Acquire a vocabulary commonly used in meetings with people from various manufacturing departments
- Recognize potential conflicts among these areas—although you may not have the expertise in each area to resolve differences or make decisions, you will know what key choices must be made in working out solutions
- Develop a business perspective of manufacturing

MODULE I

Key Competitive Challenges

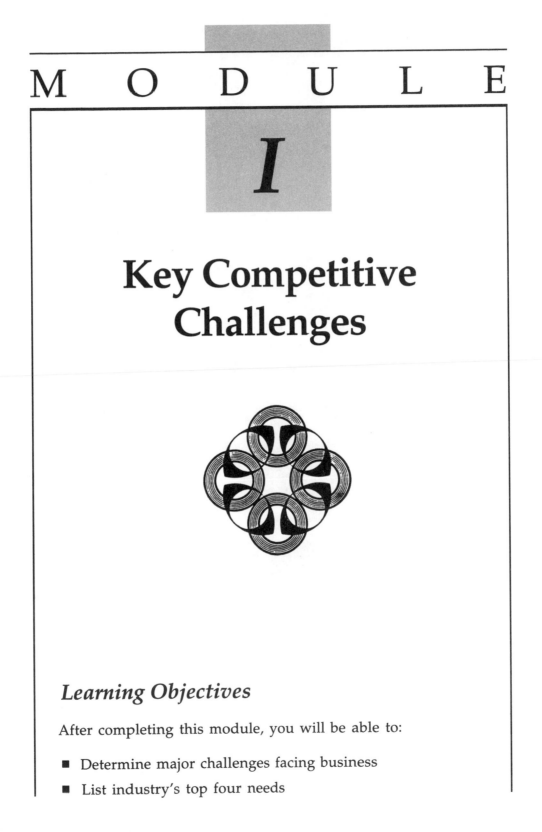

Learning Objectives

After completing this module, you will be able to:

- Determine major challenges facing business
- List industry's top four needs

THE BIG PICTURE

Key Question

What are the challenges facing business today ?

Any organization in business today is under pressure to create high-quality products, deliver products to market faster, reduce costs, increase flexibility by reacting to change, and improve its work force continually through training and education. Organizations that want to stay competitive and make a profit must accomplish these objectives. Manufacturing plays a key role in meeting these challenges.

This book helps to support these objectives by providing a fundamental knowledge of the traditional manufacturing systems—such as business planning, forecasting, master scheduling, material requirements planning, and the evolution toward a just-in-time solution.

Industry's Top Four Needs

#1 DELIVERING HIGH-QUALITY PRODUCTS

Organizations need to meet or exceed customer expectations with regard to quality. This is the true definition of **customer satisfaction.** The driving force behind quality improvement is the need to bring a quality product to market faster. The idea is to improve quality on an ongoing basis. When every process continually improves, quality improves, costs go down, profits go up and new products reach the market more quickly.

THE BIG PICTURE (continued)

#2 REDUCING COSTS

There are many ways to reduce costs. Profits grow when you decrease costs, increase revenue, or a combination of both. To maximize profits, your organization needs to reduce both tangible and intangible costs. This can be done by:

- Reducing the amount of time inventory spends under the company's ownership. This enables you to reduce other costs such as rental space, insurance to cover inventory, interest on money borrowed to pay for inventory, or computed interest on money that could have been earned. By reducing inventory and selling it faster, you improve cash flow.

- Reducing the number of decisions that must be made, as well as the number of authorizations needed once a decision has been made. You can also measure cost savings by quantifying cost reductions resulting from reducing defects and variability in processes.

- Reducing wasted time. Intangible costs are the biggest component of getting product to the customer faster. Time is wasted by unproductive meetings, telephone tag, and interruptions. More time frees you to be more productive and make more decisions.

#3 BRINGING PRODUCTS TO MARKET FASTER

Products are coming to market faster and faster, and the time to recoup the investment is getting shorter because the life of each succeeding product decreases. When you reduce the amount of time it takes to get each new product to market, you have less time in which to earn a profit. As a result, products must be profitable sooner so that the next generation of new products can be funded.

The typical product life cycle chart (birth, introduction, growth, maturity, decline, and demise) shown in Figure 1-1 demonstrates some of the issues of shorter life cycles.

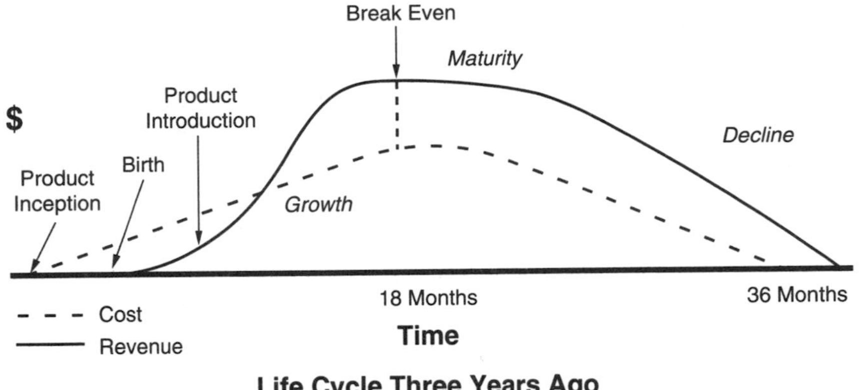

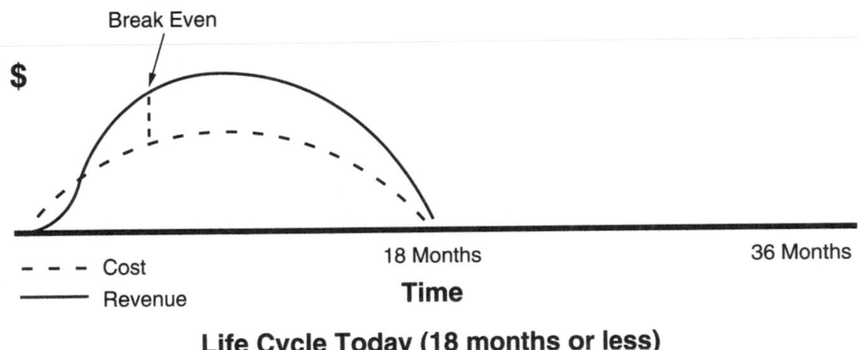

Figure 1-1: Product Life Cycle

In this example, the life cycle of products in a hypothetical industry has gone from 36 months to 18 months. Some questions for you to consider as you read through the remainder of this book are:

1. At what point should you involve the supplier?
2. How do you change the slope of the revenue curve?
3. How do you change the slope of the cost curve?

THE BIG PICTURE (continued)

The impact, if nothing is done to reduce cost significantly, is potentially devastating to the profitability of the product's lifetime. Companies are grappling with ways to change the slope of the revenue curve (up and to the left) and of the cost curve (down and to the right) by gauging success based on new measures. They include:

- **Time to market:** How fast can you get the product to market?
- **Time to volume:** How fast can you produce at a volume that attracts enough revenue to cover costs?
- **Time to profit:** How fast can you generate revenue that exceeds cost?
- **Time to change:** How fast can you make changes to accommodate customer requests and how much does the change affect your profit?

In succeeding parts of this book we show you how improvements in forecasting, master scheduling, just-in-time manufacturing, inventory management and other areas respond to all of these challenges.

#4 MAKING CHANGE FASTER AND MORE MANAGEABLE

The organizations that are best at managing change have the competitive advantage. Customers ask for faster turnaround times or other changes. You must be able to input these changes, analyze the changes and their consequences, then make decisions. You will never be able to control change, but now you can manage it. Change is manageable if your organization can anticipate change, predict change, and cause change.

► Improve Training and Education

To increase your organization's ability to respond to change, people need to be trained and educated in manufacturing theory, business and finance issues and quality control. Customers will expand their assessment and selection of your organization based not only on your products and processes, but also on your employees' education and training at all levels. Ask yourself, "What person in my organization or department would I **least** like our customers to talk to in terms of understanding quality processes?" This is the person you should educate first.

Executives at all levels in the organization have spent significant money educating their people. Unfortunately, the executives themselves often have not remained current. As a result, many find themselves making decisions about issues of which they have little or no understanding.

A major responsibility of everyone in your organization is to educate everyone else. Education and training may eventually be the only competitive weapon a company has.

► **Improve Information Systems and Networks**

Information systems are the new bottleneck. Change is happening so fast that information systems can't keep up. More advanced information systems and networks must be developed to enhance the flow of information. In order to make better decisions, you need to get information faster.

Summary

In this module the major competitive issues facing business today were discussed. It is because of these competitive issues that companies are investing more resources in these areas. Long-term planning is the topic of the next module. We will be discussing these competetive issues throughout the rest of the book.

Module 1 Exercises

Answer the following questions.

1. Briefly describe two major issues facing business today.

____
____
____
____
____
____

2. How is change affecting your company?

____
____
____
____
____
____

3. How do you think you can manage change?

____
____
____
____
____
____

M O D U L E

II

Long-Term Planning

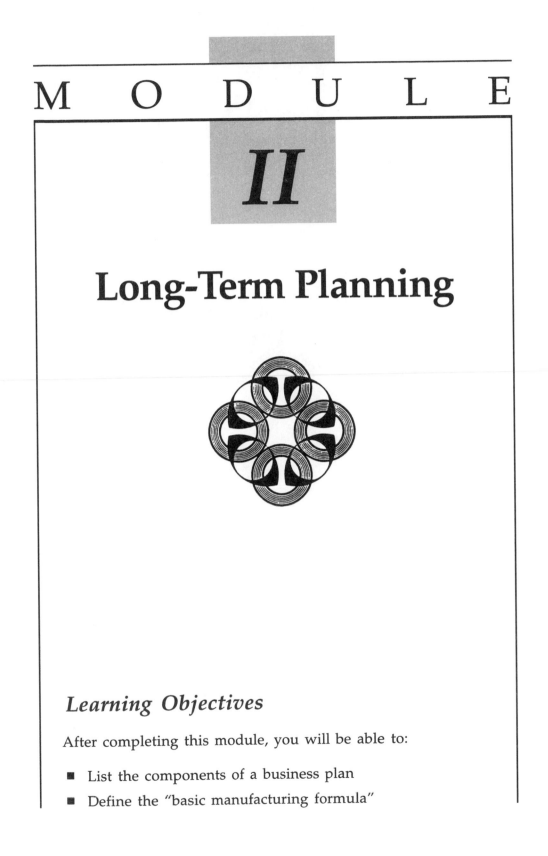

Learning Objectives

After completing this module, you will be able to:

- List the components of a business plan
- Define the "basic manufacturing formula"

LONG-TERM PLANNING

"The best way to predict the future is to plan it.

—Peter Drucker
Management Consultant

The planning process is organized by periods of time into the following general categories. While experts disagree as to the relative length of each category, for purposes of this book we will use the following:

Long-term planning	1 to 5 years
Medium-term planning	3 to 18 months
Short-term planning	1 to 60 days

In business, these planning periods overlap and companies will place varying degrees of emphasis on each period.

Two of the outcomes of long-term planning activities are a manufacturing strategy and an annual production plan that drives the master schedule. The diagram on page 12 gives you a sense of the bigger picture and shows you where you are in the planning process. Figure 2-1 illustrates the activities involved in long-term planning.

USE THE FOLLOWING FLOWCHART
TO TRACK YOUR PLANNING . . .

LONG-TERM PLANNING (continued)

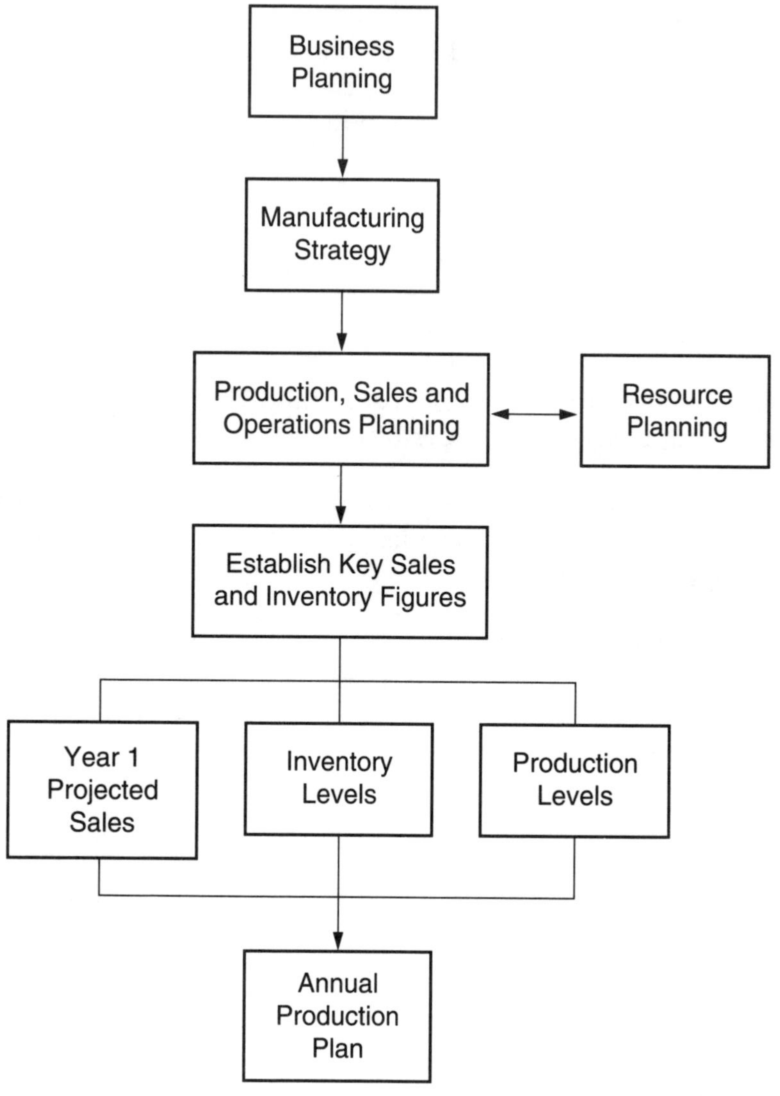

Figure 2-1: Long-Term Planning

ESTABLISH A BUSINESS PLAN

Key Question

What is your business today, and what will it be in the future?

A **business plan** is a statement of long-range strategy supported by projection of resources. Business plans are important because they describe what the business looks like today and predict what it will look like in the future. This plan sets the direction for the company. It also creates a framework in which the organization can respond to changes required to stay competitive. To give all employees a sense of where the company is headed, appropriate excerpts should be communicated to all levels of the organization; however, any competitive, sensitive information would require limited distribution.

Most organizations have a business plan. If you don't have access to this plan, or if your organization does not have a business plan, then it would be good practice to develop one of your own. By developing your own business plan, you will gain valuable experience to add to your portfolio of skills.

Components of a Business Plan

The following are components of a business plan. Some of these components are commonly found in business plans; some are not typically included but should be considered.

Mission Statement

Objectives

Customers

Products and Services

Competition

Current Economic Environment

Distribution Channels

Production/Sales and Operation Plan (including the Resource Plan)

Financial Analysis

Major Processes

Continuous Process Improvement (CPI) Program

Functional Strategies

Training and Education Strategy

Potential Problems

Recommendations and plan of action to Implement Them

ESTABLISH A BUSINESS PLAN (continued)

Business plans may be as brief as a few pages or quite lengthy. In general, a business plan should be only as long as necessary to cover each topic. Also, business plans are meant to be updated because your business is continually changing.

You may develop the components indicated above in a different sequence. Developing a business plan is an iterative process, however, and you will need to re-examine each component and make adjustments before completing a final draft.

FORMULATE YOUR MANUFACTURING STRATEGY

The **manufacturing strategy** is one of the most important strategies because it includes the assumptions required to support the long-term sales portion of the overall business plan. If you have access to your organization's business plan, you should review it and use it as the basis to formulate a strategy for yourself, your own functional organization, department or work group.

Your manufacturing strategy should support the business plan and detail the following:

- Dealing with long-term market trends
- Projected growth and variability of demand
- The emergence of new technologies
- The emergence of new organization structures
- The role of information technology
- The impact of capital investment in light of shorter product life cycles
- Key competitive issues, such as time to market, time to volume, quality, costing and managing change faster and faster

An important component of the manufacturing strategy is a description of the plan to be used to manage each supplier. This description should answer these questions:

- What are the supplier-management objectives?
- What strategy will be used with each supplier to ensure that supplier management objectives are met?

INITIATE PRODUCTION PLANNING

Key Question

What is the overall level of manufacturing required to meet the projected sales and inventory levels

The **production plan** sets the overall level of manufacturing output by year needed to meet the planned levels of sales and of inventory. The manufacturing output levels reflect the company's objectives as documented in the business plan. The production plan acts as a control and constraint to the master production schedule (MPS). The master schedule shows when shipments are expected to occur and the capacity that will be required by people and machines.

The purpose of the production plan is to:

- Establish the overall level of manufacturing output the company plans to produce (normally stated in units, cost of sales and sales dollar output)

- Authorize break down of the production plan into specific end items and end products in the MPS

- Assist the company in planning what resources it requires

- Stabilize production and employment

The result of the production plan is that the company can project production by year over the life of the business plan (for example, 1–5 years). The plan is developed during the production planning process and must be agreed upon by marketing, manufacturing, R&D, and finance, as well as other appropriate functional groups. The plan states the anticipated rate of production in aggregate terms, usually by product family. It covers families or groups of products built by a common manufacturing organization.

During the production planning process, the production plan is compared to the long-term resource plan to ensure that there are enough resources—such as facilities, equipment, people, materials, and cash—to fund this growth. The process of determining the amount of resources (capacity) available is called **resource planning.**

Establish Key Sales and Inventory Figures

Key Question

How do you determine how manufacturing can manage inventory and produce the products necessary to meet sales plan goals for the first year ?

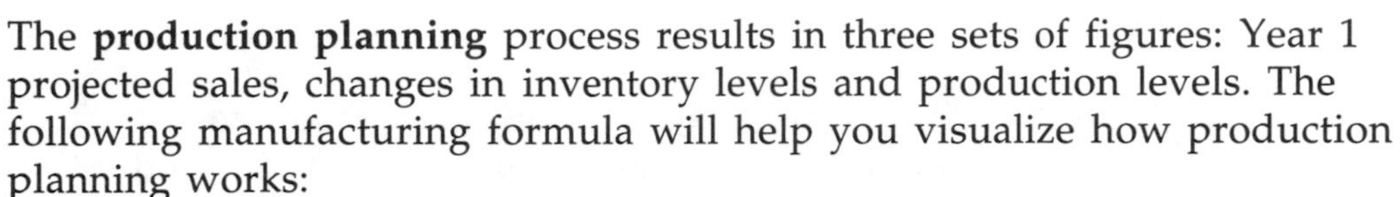

The **production planning** process results in three sets of figures: Year 1 projected sales, changes in inventory levels and production levels. The following manufacturing formula will help you visualize how production planning works:

Step	Basic Manufacturing Formula		Units
4		Beginning Inventory	1,000
5	+	Production (Build Plan)	9,500
3	=	Available Inventory to Ship	10,500
1	–	Shipments/Sales	10,000
2	=	Ending Inventory	500

INITIATE PRODUCTION PLANNING (continued)

The steps for determining the numbers in the basic manufacturing formula are described as follows.

STEP 1 First you need to establish projected shipments/sales for the year. Your top executives establish the sales required to meet the business objectives for growth, market share and so on. In this example, the projected shipment is 10,000 units.

STEP 2 Next, you must set ending inventory levels. Inventory levels are based on two requirements:

- The desired customer level of satisfaction. (How many times can you ship when the customer wants the product shipped?) This topic will be discussed in detail in the next module.
- Forecast error, which refers to the difference between forecasted sales and actual sales (fluctuation in demand).

In this example, the projected (forecasted) ending inventory level is 500 units.

STEP 3 When you have determined the desired level of shipments and have projected the ending inventory levels, you can determine the available inventory units to ship by adding the shipment of 10,000 units to the projected ending inventory level of 500 units. The available inventory to ship is equal to 10,500 units.

STEP 4 The beginning inventory for the year is taken directly from the ending inventory of the previous year. In this example, it is a given 1,000 units.

STEP 5 You can now determine the production for the year by subtracting the beginning inventory (1,000 units) from the available-to-ship inventory (10,500 units). In this example, the production is 9,500 units.

Business planning and production planning are iterative processes that are conducted at the highest levels of the organization. These are ongoing activities that receive the most attention when the organization is planning for the next year's budget. Projecting sales for the coming year is a vital part of business and production planning because projected sales determine how much revenue the organization will need in order to meet the business plan objectives, such as market share and competitive status.

Identify Adequate Resources

To have enough capacity to meet existing sales levels for the present year and the next four years, you must have adequate resources. If you find there won't be enough capacity, you will either have to increase capacity or revise the sales plan.

DETERMINE RESOURCE PLANNING

Key Question

Do you have enough resources to meet the production plan?

To produce (build) the projected sales levels and changes in inventory levels for the coming year, you must do adequate **resource planning** in order to acquire the appropriate people, equipment and material from suppliers. In the long-term you may even need to acquire buildings and land.

If there are not enough resources, you must make adjustments to fund additional acquisition or you must revise the sales plan or inventory levels. In practice you will probably combine these two alternatives. The process of determining if enough resources are available is an iterative one that is driven by executives down through the organization.

Accurate and complete resource plans, combined with thorough data on resource availability, allow management to set realistic production rates that are consistent with the business plan. Resource planning takes into account which resources require long lead-times to acquire and require top management approval.

Figure 2-2 is an example of how the long-term planning activities of business planning, production planning, resource planning and master production scheduling tie together.

LONG-TERM BUSIENSS PLANNING—
TYING IT ALL TOGETHER

• Mission Statement
• Objectives
• Customers
• Productions & Services
• Competition
• Current Economic Env.
• Distribution Channels
• Production, Sales and Ops Plan
• Financial Analysis
Business Planning
• Major Processes
• CPI Program
• Functional Strategies: Supplier Management Strategy
• Training & Educational Strategy
• Potential Problems
• Recommendations
• Implementation Action Plan
R&D Strategy
Marketing Strategy
Manufacturing Strategy
Sales Strategy
Finance Strategy
Production Planning (Production, Sales and Operation Plan)
Basic Manufacturing Formula
Beginning Inventory
+ Production Plan
= Available to Ship
– Projected Sales
= Ending Inventory
Resource Planning
People
Equipment
Facilities
Land
Supplies/Suppliers
Capital
Master Production Schedule (MPS)
MPS Product A Production Line
MPS Product B Production Line
Basic Manufacturing Formula
Beginning Inventory
+ Production Plan
= Available to Ship
– MPS (Ship)
= Ending Inventory
Testing the Production Plan
Rough-Cut Capacity Planning
Customer Order

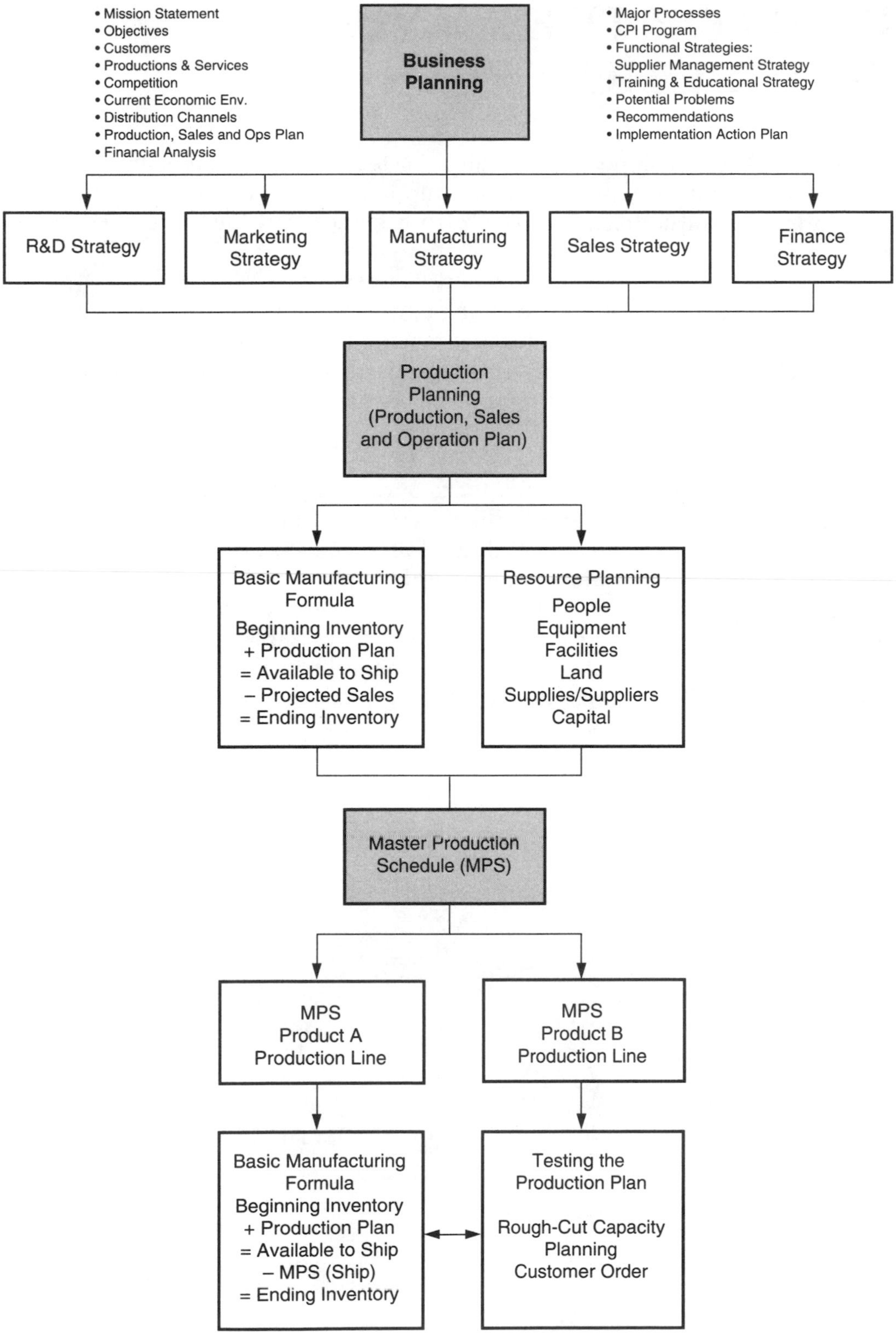

Figure 2-2: Long-Term Planning

DEVELOP THE ANNUAL PRODUCTION PLAN

The result of establishing the annual projected sales, and the subsequent changes in inventory levels to enable shipments to be timely, is documented in an **annual production plan.** This plan assumes that there are adequate resources.

The annual production plan shows the aggregate level of production, which provides the basis for authorizing the master production schedule(s). The master schedule represents the breaking apart of the company-wide production plan into specific product families and/or products. The master schedule will be discussed in Module 3.

Before you complete this module, make sure you thoroughly understand the basic manufacturing formula discussed previously. The following formula has been expanded to include dollar values. This formula is one that accountants must make certain is in balance at the end of every month, quarter, and year in order to receive a clean audit report. The two versions of the basic manufacturing formula—units and dollars—are not often tied together. The unit amount multiplied by the appropriate unit cost should tie closely to the dollar figures, thus providing a check-and-balance situation between units and dollars.

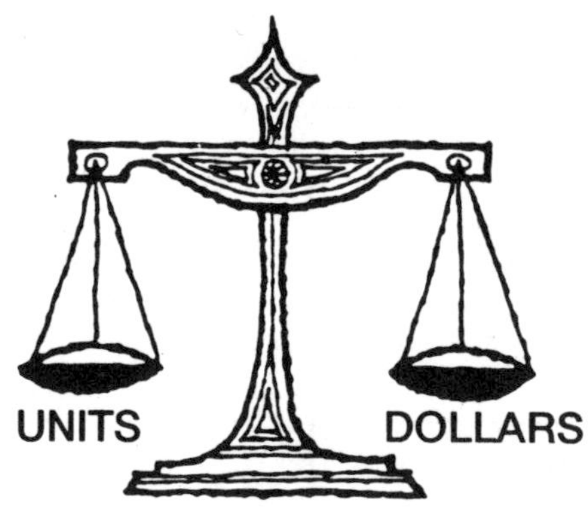

Summary

This module introduced you to the activities involved in long-term planning, including business planning, production planning and resource planning. You were also introduced to the basic manufacturing formula and its purpose. The next module discusses medium-term planning activities. You will learn about the master schedule and the tools and techniques required to produce an effective schedule. Following is an overview of the upcoming modules.

Basic Manufacturing Formula	Units	Dollars	Tools/Techniques
Beginning Inventory	1,000	1,000	From last year's audited financial statement
+ Production (Build Plan)	9,500	9,500	• Resource Requirement Plan • Rated Capacity calculation • Just-in-Time (JIT) manufacturing • Material requirement planning (MRP)
= Available Inventory to Ship	10,500	10,500	
– Shipments/Sales	10,000	10,000	• Customer orders (lead-time management) • Forecast: —Forecast error —Customer service level/probability
= Ending Inventory	500	500	• ABC/Classification

Module 2 Exercise

Please answer the following questions. *See pages 105–106 in the back of the book for the answers.*

1. Define the following terms.

Business plan: ____________________

Manufacturing strategy: ____________________

Production planning: ____________________

Production plan: ____________________

Resource plan: ____________________

2. List five components of a business plan.

3. State the basic manufacturing formula:

4. A planner for ABC Company is developing a production plan. The demand and production rates for the company for the next four periods are shown below.

Given that the beginning inventory at the start of Period 1 is 200 units, calculate the beginning inventory, ending inventory, average inventory, and back orders, if any, for each of the other periods.

Remember, the ending inventory for one period becomes the beginning inventory for the next period.

	Period			
Basic Manufacturing Formula	**1**	**2**	**3**	**4**
Beginning Inventory	200			
+ Production Requirement	3,800	6,000	4,100	6,000
= Available Products to Sell				
– Projected Sales	4,000	4,500	2,200	6,400
= Ending Inventory				
Average Inventory				

Note: Average inventory = (Beginning inventory + Ending inventory) ÷ 2.

MODULE

III

Medium-Term Planning

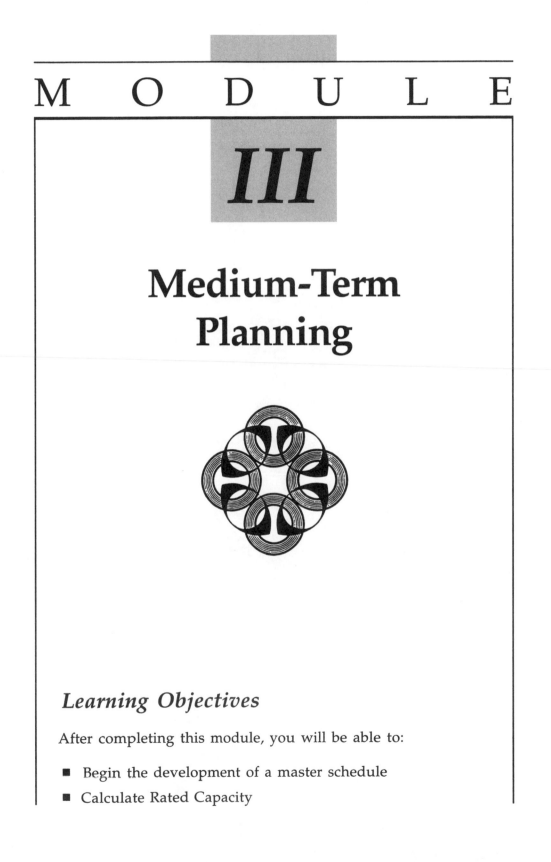

Learning Objectives

After completing this module, you will be able to:

- Begin the development of a master schedule
- Calculate Rated Capacity

MEDIUM-TERM PLANNING

The last module covered the business plan, supported by a manufacturing strategy and details such as revenue and cost projections for five years or more.

In this module, the first year's portion of the business plan is the basis for discussing the planning required to execute the master schedule. The master schedule gives dates when products will be shipped to customers.

The theory of the master planning process and the importance of forecasting are discussed in detail. Inventory and capacity planning are highlighted, then combined with the basic manufacturing formula to provide a system of checks and balances, integrated horizontally over the business planning and vertically through the next year's annual plan. The annual plan can be broken down by days, weeks, months and quarters, depending on the level of detail required.

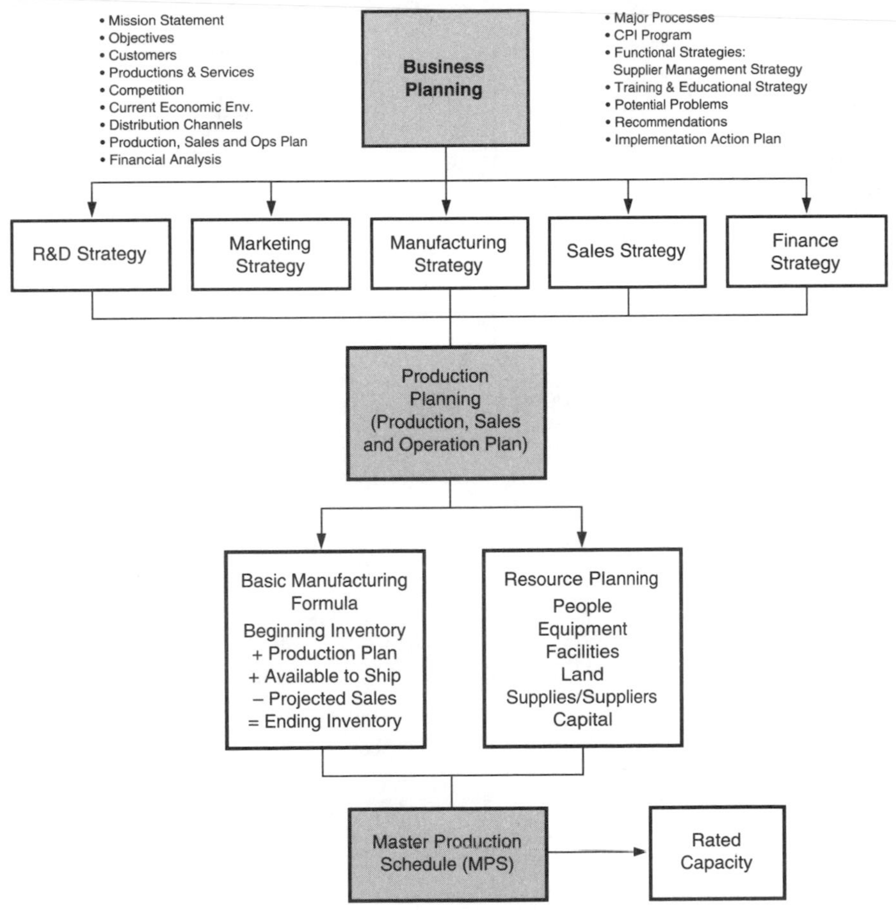

Figure 3-1: Long-Term Planning

MEDIUM-TERM PLANNING (continued)

Medium-term planning involves scheduling master production and managing demand.

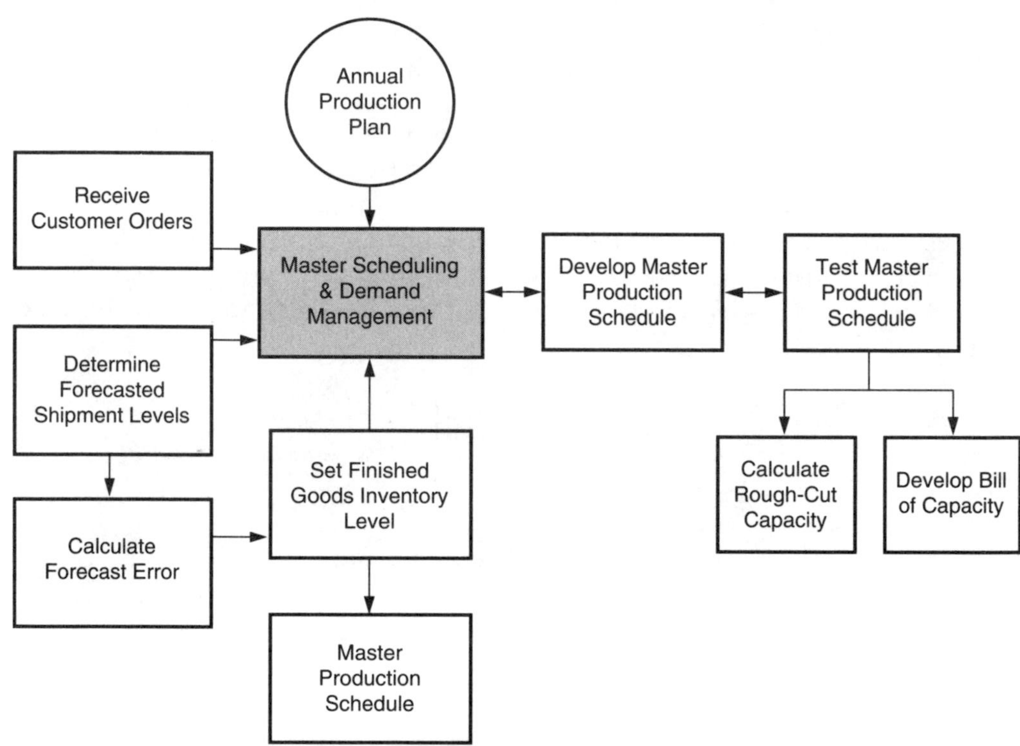

Figure 3-2: Medium-Term Planning

ACTIVATE MASTER SCHEDULING AND DEMAND MANAGEMENT

Key Question

How much must be produced to meet the shipment levels and level of inventory to satisfy customers? ?

The annual production plan, which is the result of the long-term planning process, drives the master schedule (or individual master schedules, depending on the number of business units or divisions). Master scheduling and demand management are planning processes that result in the development of a **master production schedule** (MPS), which must be tested before it is implemented. The MPS is a line in the master schedule that shows how many products must be produced and on what dates.

Master Schedule

The **master schedule** uses customer orders, forecasts (shipment levels), rough-cut capacity planning and inventory levels (beginning and ending) established to meet desired customer-service objectives. *The master schedule is a commitment to ship on a specified date and a commitment of capacity. It is a time-phased planning process.*

In addition to forecasts and customer orders, this schedule contains the available-to-promise and projected available inventory balances. The output of the master schedule is the line called the MPS. The amounts on this line are used to drive the material requirements plan, which is covered in the next module. In this module the material requirement plan (MRP) covers the scheduling of manufacturing the parts required to build the products for customers who are included in the master schedule. Figure 3–3 on page 32 is an example of a master schedule.

ACTIVATE MASTER SCHEDULING AND DEMAND MANAGEMENT (continued)

Master Schedule

Item: 1645ASTER
Desciption: Magic Pen
Planning Horizon: 6 months

Period	**1**	**2**	**3**	**4**	**5**	**6**
Forecast	360	420	340	340	240	280
Customer Orders	380	400	300	400	120	400
Projected Available Balance (Inventory) 800	420	20	720	320	1080	680
Available-to-Promise	20		300		480	
Master Production Schedule			1000		1000	

▼ ▼
Explosion into MRP

Figure 3-3: Typical Master Production Schedule

Master Scheduling includes demand management (forecasting, service orders, master scheduling [including final assembly scheduling]) and **rough-cut capacity planning,** which provides a check on capacity to meet the independent demand in the master schedule. Master schedule item (and description) is the product that will be shipped to the customer. It may include service or repair parts.

FORECAST SHIPMENT LEVELS

Key Question

In order to meet the coming year's revenue plan, what shipment levels must be achieved?

The forecasted sales are usually stated as a monthly rate. For planning purposes, the rate must be expressed in units identical to those in the production plan. Some master schedules will also include the dollar amounts of the forecasted sales. The sales forecast represents sales and marketing management's best estimate of future orders. Customer orders and forecasts of future customer orders, when combined, equal the shipment levels for the coming periods (for example, months, quarters, years).

Forecasting is critical to estimating future demand. This estimate may be developed by using mathematical formulas, data from informal sources or a combination of both. Forecasting is key to all aspects of a successful business-planning system. As customers place more demands or require faster deliveries, your ability to forecast as accurately as possible is essential.

For forecasts to be usable, they must be based on timely data gathered in a consistent manner. A good forecasting process must include the use of forecasting tools, the creation and collection of information, the management of this information and finally the making of well-informed decisions about what you need to produce. Forecasting is meaningful only if it helps to improve customer service, reduce inventory, increase productivity and improve the deliveries from suppliers.

Every good forecast includes an estimate of the forecast error. The forecast error is the difference between what you thought you were going to ship and what you actually shipped. In order to improve sales forecasts, you will first need to calculate the forecast error (actual sales minus forecasted sales equals forecast error).

FORECAST SHIPMENT LEVELS (continued)

	1	2	3	
Item	**Actual**	**Forecast**	**Forecast Error**	**% Forecast Error**
Product A	245	230	+15	+6.5%
Product F	110	120	–10	–8.3
Total	**355**	**350**	**+5**	**+1.4%**

Figure 3-4: Year 2—Division A Products

The numbers over the columns in the example above represent column numbers. The entries below tell you what to do when you enter your own figures.

COLUMN	WHAT TO DO
1	Enter actual sales figures from the sales report.
2	Enter forecast figures from your final forecast.
3	Calculate the forecast error for each period by subtracting column 2 from column 1.

In this example, the combined forecast error for Products A and F is equal to +1.4 percent. Marketing people would measure their success based on the total forecast error of 1.4 percent, whereas manufacturing people would build products based on the individual product demand, and therefore would be affected by the forecast errors of each product. The forecast error can be averaged over the history of earlier years to serve as the basis for determining what level of inventory you must carry to ensure a certain probability of shipping to a customer on time.

The more accurate your individual product sales forecasting is, the smaller your forecast error and the less inventory you'll have to carry to maintain a specified level of customer service. By carrying less inventory, you can use the capacity of machines required to build the products more effectively. You are not building inventory before you need it, and thus committing capacity of machines too early. By carrying less inventory, you generally use less space, and don't use space too early.

Develop a Forecast Model

There are many forecasting tools and techniques you can use to improve your forecasts. The tools and techniques must be part of an overall system that allows for changes in demand and is supported by policies that set guidelines to respond to these changes.

Improved forecasting models can reduce the amount of forecast error. Reducing error means you can reduce the inventory maintained to absorb the forecast error. This results in less inventory, fewer stockouts, and so on. Reduced forecast error also gives you more flexibility in using machine capacity.

Simple forecasting models frequently provide results that are nearly as good as the more complex ones. The more elaborate mathematical models are useful only if nontechnical users can understand them and make appropriate decisions based on the results.

The advantage of simple models is that they can be understood by a greater number of people, are less expensive to implement and can be applied in the wide number of cases required in production. Few inventory items, few finished products, and very few management standards are important enough to justify the expense of elaborate forecasting models.

Approaches to Forecasting

Forecasting techniques and tools are either qualitative (relying on judgment) or quantitative (relying on data). Quantitative techniques are either intrinsic or extrinsic. Intrinsic forecasting relies solely on the historical data of the item being forecast. Extrinsic forecasting relies on historical data of items or events related to that item. In practice, your final forecast model may combine both qualitative and quantitative techniques.

FORECAST SHIPMENT LEVELS (continued)

Master Schedule

Item: 1645ASTER
Desciption: Magic Pen
1. **Planning Horizon:** 6 months

Period	**1**	**2**	**3**	**4**	**5**	**6**
Forecast	360	420	340	340	240	280
Customer Orders	380	400	300	400	120	400
2. Projected Available Balance (Inventory) 800	420	20	720	320	1080	680
3. Available-to-Promise	20		300		480	
4. Master Production Schedule			1000		1000	

▼ ▼
Explosion into MRP

Line 1: Planning horizon is the period of time into which the master schedule extends. The length of a forecast horizon is primarily determined by the purpose of the forecast. At a minimum, the planning horizon will extend as long as the lead-time of the longest lead-time item, plus the time it takes to make changes to capacity because of schedule changes.

Line 2: Projected available balance, also known as inventory on hand, is the amount of inventory a company decides to carry to ensure that customer needs will be satisfied.

Line 3: Available-to-promise is the line in the Master Schedule that shows the amount of product that has not been committed to customer orders.

Line 4: The Master Production Schedule shows the quantities of products that need to be built. (In the example, it would be 1000 units of the product in periods 3 and 5.) These amounts would drive MRP.

Figure 3-5: Typical Master Production Schedule

TEST THE MASTER PRODUCTION SCHEDULE

Key Question

Is there enough capacity to meet the committed ship dates in the MPS ?

The master schedule must be realistic. This means that before you commit to customer orders, the MPS must be tested within the capacity constraints of the production facility. In this context, capacity is defined in terms of output per machine or person per shift. Without sufficient capacity, customer delivery dates may be missed.

#1 Develop a Bill of Capacity

The **bill of capacity** shows how much labor and machine time are required to produce the typical unit of a product. When you multiply the capacity required to produce the typical unit times the units required by the MPS, you have the total estimated units per period.

#2 Calculate Rough-Cut Capacity

Rough-cut capacity planning (RCCP), also known as resource requirement planning, is the process of converting the MPS into capacity needs for key resources: people, equipment, facilities, suppliers' capabilities and money required to fund acquisitions. The purpose of RCCP is to establisthe feasibility of master production schedule.

TEST THE MASTER PRODUCTION SCHEDULE (continued)

Rated Capacity Formula

There is a formula that calculates how much each machine and/or person can produce in an hour, day, week, etc. This formula or calculation is called **rated capacity.**

Rated Capacity = *Machines and/or people*

× *Hours per shift*

× *Shifts per day*

× *Efficiency*

× *Utilization**

× *Days per week, month, etc.*

= *Standard Hours*

× *Units per hour*

= *Units per day, week, month*

*Reasons for not utilizing equipment/machines during an 8-hour shift include:

- Planned maintenance
- Unplanned maintenance
- Set-up
- Absenteeism
- Meetings
- Material shortages
- Lack of customer orders
- Material defects

The result of the rated-capacity is compared to the forecast projected inventory levels and customer orders in the master schedule. If there is enough capacity to produce the units committed in the master schedule, the master schedule will be implemented. If there is not enough capacity, adjustments to the master schedule or the capacity will have to be made.

Summary

Module three emphasized the importance of forecasting. You were introduced to the following: the master schedule, customer orders, the forecast, projected available balance and available to promise. Rough-cut capacity planning, which provides a check on capacity to meet the independent demand in the master schedule, was discussed in detail. In addition you learned about the master production schedule and its impact on the material plan. The material planning process, also known as material requirements planning, is covered in the next module.

The portion of the manufacturing formula and the related tools and techniques covered in this module are indicated as follows.

Basic Manufacturing Formula	Units	Dollars	Tools/Techniques
Beginning Inventory	1,000	1,000	From last year's audited financial statement
+ Production (Build Plan)	9,500	9,500	• Resource Requirement Plan • Rated Capacity calculation • Just-in-Time (JIT) manufacturing • Material requirement planning (MRP)
= Available Inventory to Ship	10,500	10,500	
– Shipments/Sales	10,000	10,000	• Customer orders (lead-time management) • Forecast: —Forecast error —Customer service level/probability
= Ending Inventory	500	500	• ABC/Classification

Module 3 Exercise

In this exercise you will determine capacity and identify the bottleneck work center. The answers are on pages 107–108 in the back of the book.

1. Using the following formula, recalculate the rated capacity (work-center capacity hours) for work centers 700, 750, and 400.

Using the same formula, calculate rated capacity for work centers 020, 500, and 550.

Formula for Determining Rated Capacity

(shifts per day) × (machines or work stations) × (hours per shift) × (utilization) × (efficiency) = standard hours per day per work center capacity

Assumptions: 8 working hours, 1 shift

					1	2	3	4
Work Center Number	**Work Center Descrip.**	**Number of Machines**	**Machine Use**	**Efficiency**	**Work Center Capacity in Hrs per Day**	**Units per Hours**	**Units per Day**	**Units per 20-day Month**
700	Dip Insertion	2	.90	.90	12.96	5		
750	Axiel Insertion	4	.90	.85	24.48	7		
400	Cut & Clinch	6	.85	1.10	44.88	5		
020	Wave Solder	1	.90	.90		5		
500	Automated Test Equipment	3	.80	1.05		6		
550	Functional Test	2	.90	1.00		4		

COLUMN	WHAT TO DO
2	This information has been provided for you, based on engineering estimates and history.
3	Multiply column 1 by column 2.
4	Multiply column 3 by 20 work days.

2. If the MPS calls for shipping 1,200 units: identify the bottleneck work center(s), if any.______________________________

3. Suggest how you would increase the bottleneck work center's capacity.

- Long-Term: (1–5 years)

  ____

  ____

- Medium-Term (30–360 days)

  ____

  ____

- Short-Term: (next 30 days)

  ____

  ____

4. Test your understanding by filling in the blanks.

____________________ + ____________________ = shipment levels for coming periods.

5. Forecasting helps the manufacturer to

____________________ ____________________

____________________ ____________________

6. What is the rated capacity formula?

______________________________ ×

______________________________ ×

______________________________ ×

______________________________ ×

______________________________ ×

= ______________________________

MODULE

IV

Short-Term Planning Phase I: Material Control

Learning Objectives

After completing this module, you will be able to:

- Use the gross-to-net-requirement formula
- Explain the reason for establishing a parent/component relationship

SHORT-TERM PLANNING

Module 3 examined the current year's portion of the business plan and explained the master scheduling process. This module discusses the additional planning required to execute the tactics to meet the plan.

The following modules cover the theory of material and capacity requirements and inventory management, and ties the process of manufacturing products into the financial system that is necessary to the decision-making process. It describes tools such as MRP spreadsheets that support the understanding of material requirements plan (MRP) logic.

Short-term planning involves: material control, production activity control, evolution to just-in-time manufacturing (JIT), and inventory control. Figure 4-1 on page 46 illustrates the specific activities involved in each of these phases.

SHORT-TERM PLANNING (continued)

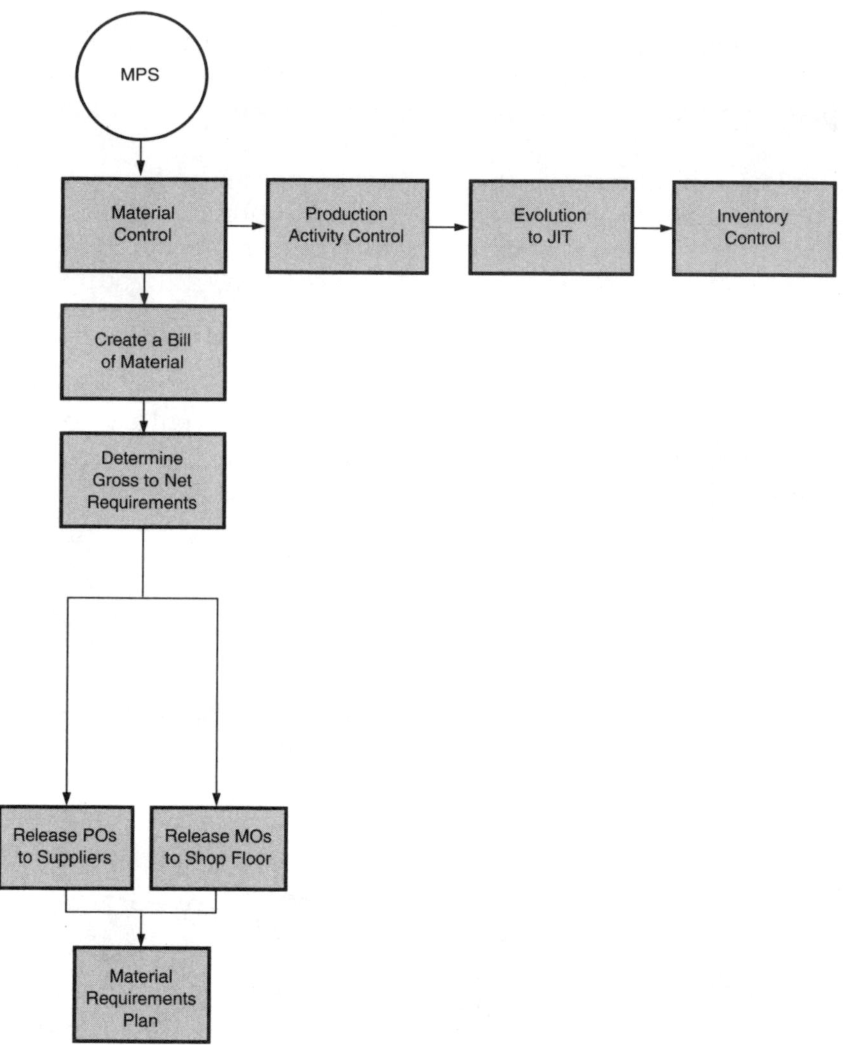

Figure 4-1: Short-Term Planning

IMPLEMENT MATERIAL REQUIREMENTS PLANNING

Material requirements planning (MRP) uses information from the master production schedule (MPS) to schedule the right part, at the right time, in the right place. The material requirements plan suggests how to release and reprioritize orders and generates reports that make suggestions for the cycle counts. MRP also provides data to support priority planning and capacity requirements planning, as well as scheduling, dispatching, and purchasing systems.

MRP is driven by input from the MPS. The product of the MPS is derived primarily from the forecast, customer orders, spare part and service requirements, interdivision orders, new product requirements and perhaps even special marketing promotions. If an item is not included in the master schedule, the parts needed to build it cannot be scheduled by the MRP.

The MRP schedules requirements for all the component parts. These are combined to develop the gross requirements for each part. An MRP system suggests inventory levels over a specified period of time, order policies, bills of material explosions, and the time-phased planning of the release of material to be built on the shop floor or purchased from suppliers and contractors.

The reports generated by MRP provide decision-making tools for the placement and rescheduling of manufacturing orders and purchase orders.

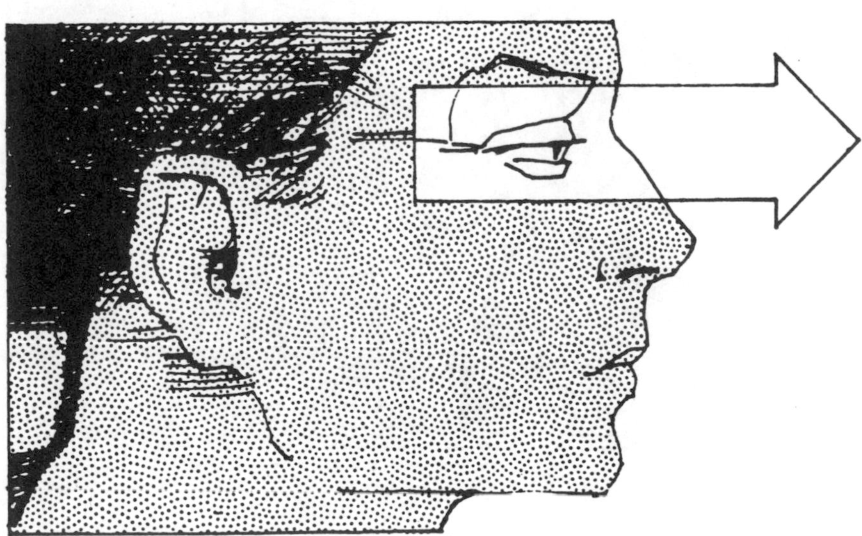

IMPLEMENT MATERIAL REQUIREMENTS PLANNING (continued)

MRP Techniques

MRP addresses the nature of demand and determines how planned material supply will satisfy that demand. Planning for material includes generating net requirements and maintaining priorities.

The term "component item" in MRP covers the scheduling of all parts required to make the end items called for by the MPS. Component items can include raw material, semi-finished and piece parts, subassemblies and so on. The master schedule (independent demand) creates the dependent demand from a **bill of material** (BOM) (which lists the parts and quantities required to build each item) and explodes into the MRP.

A subassembly or component is a raw material, ingredient or part used at a higher level to make up an assembly. Subassemblies or components include everything that is part of MRP.

CREATE A BILL OF MATERIAL

When there is demand for an end item, and you've decided to build it, you will need to schedule material by following the MRP process.

Parent/Component Relationship (Structuring the BOM)

A BOM contains a list of parts and quantities required to build an end item. The establishment of the relationship between the end item and its parts, called "structuring the BOM," is done systematically through a process of establishing the parent-component relationship.

BOM structuring is the process that organizes BOMs and results in the subassemblies that go into assemblies and then become part of the end product. Each parent-component relationship establishes links between the end item and its parts or between two or more parts. Figure 4-2 on page 50 shows a BOM structure with parents and components.

Product Structure Levels

Every part in a product structure is given a code indicating the level in which that part is used within the BOM. It is a common practice to designate the end item/product as level 0. The subsequent assemblies, subassemblies, and raw materials are assigned levels 1, 2, and so on down through the product structure. The MRP system uses this product structure to explode downward, level by level. The lowest level in which an item is structured in the BOM is called its low-level code. The MRP logic requires the establishment of the low-level code when it is calculating part requirements.

CREATE A BILL OF MATERIAL (continued)

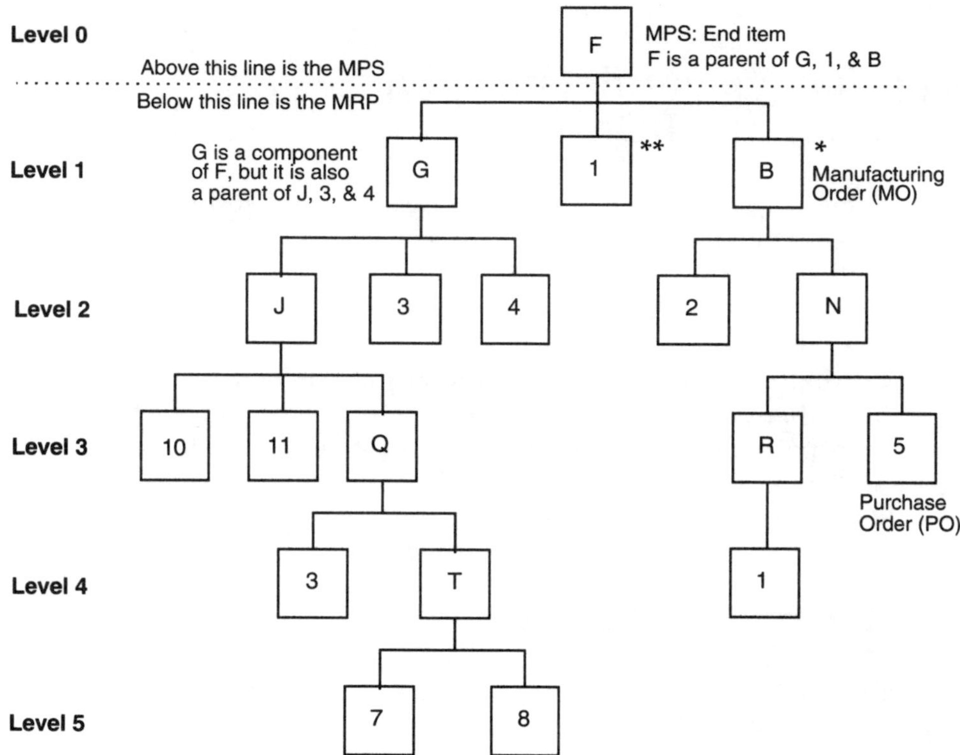

*A manufacturing order (work order) would be required to build part B.

**A purchase order would be needed to acquire parts 3 and 4. As a rule of thumb, whenever there are no components to the part, a purchase order is required.

Note: For purposes of this book, subassemblies or any component built internally will have part numbers that begin with alphabetical characters. Purchase part numbers will begin with numerical characters.

Figure 4-2: BOM Structure

DETERMINE GROSS-TO-NET REQUIREMENTS

Key Question

How is the independent demand contained in the MPS translated to the dependent demand contained in the MRP

The MPS uses the information contained in a BOM to create the MRP explosion. The term explosion in this context means going from one level to the next in the BOM (such as level "0" to level "1").

The following figure shows a simplified sequence that the master schedule and MRP would follow in order to translate independent demand into dependent demand. Each of these terms is discussed in detail below.

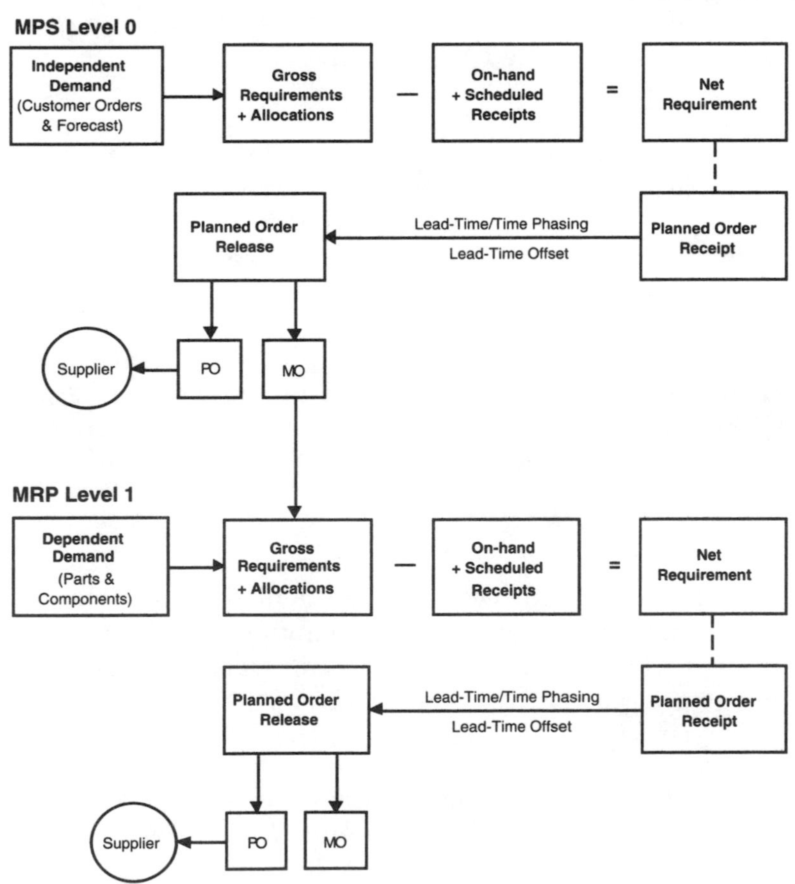

Figure 4-3: Process for Determining Gross-to-Net Requirements

DETERMINE GROSS-TO-NET REQUIREMENTS (continued)

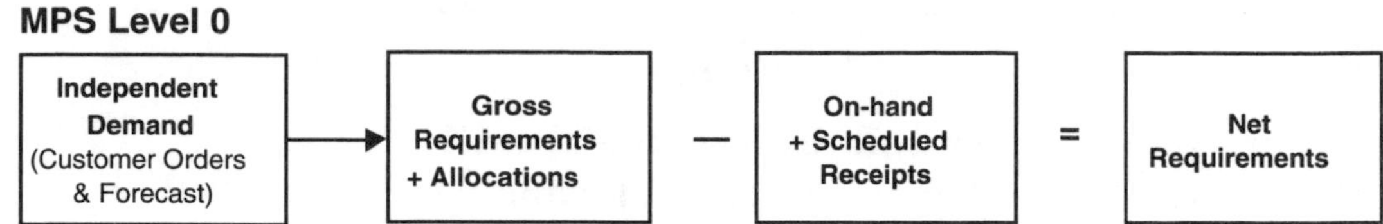

Independent Demand—Independent demand comes from sources such as the forecast, customer orders for end items and repair parts, and orders from other divisions of your company. Independent demand is demand for an end item or service part that is unrelated to the demand for other items. The MPS contains only independent demand.

Gross requirements—Gross requirements are the total dependent and/or independent requirements for a product or part prior to accounting for the item currently on hand or scheduled to be received.

Allocations—The allocation process reserves for manufacturing orders parts that have not been released to the shop floor from the warehouse. An allocation creates a picking list that goes to the warehouse. The allocated part may not be sent from the warehouse until later, so an allocation ensures that the part will not be used to fill another order.

On-hand Inventory—On hand inventory is the quantity which is physically located in stock, shown in the inventory records as being physically in stock. Periodically, this on-hand inventory is reconciled to the financial inventory (book inventory).

Scheduled Receipts—Scheduled receipts are orders already released (opened) either to manufacturing (production, manufacturing, or shop orders), or to suppliers. Receipts released in a prior planning period are scheduled to arrive during the subsequent planning.

Net Requirements—The **net requirements** are order amounts that remain after one subtracts on-hand and scheduled receipts from gross requirements and allocations.

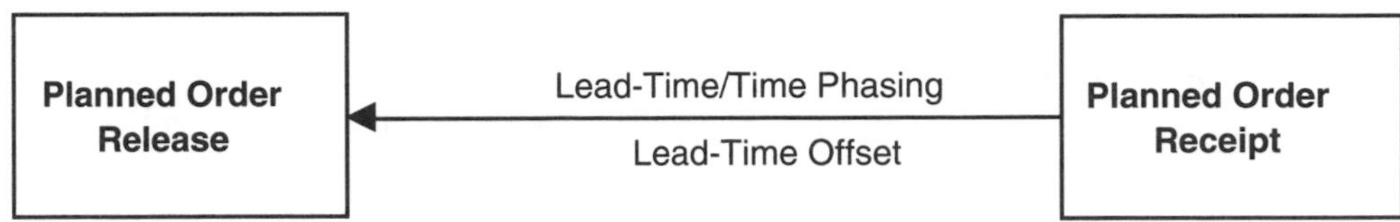

Planned Order Receipt—When there is a net requirement, you must plan to receive an order to satisfy it. If you do not, a material shortage will result. A planned order receipt is the quantity you plan to receive at a future date. Planned order receipts differ from scheduled receipts in that they may change during subsequent planning periods. Scheduled receipts on the other hand, have been built or are in the process of being built, either by suppliers or internally. Changes to the schedule receipts are very costly.

Lead-Time—In order to receive an order, you need to determine the amount of time it takes to receive the order from your manufacturing floor or from the supplier. This length of time is called lead-time. The major components of lead time are *queue* (the time the inventory is sitting on the shop floor waiting to be worked on), *set-up* (time spent preparing the machine), *run time* (time the machine is actually running), *wait* (time for the item to be moved to the next machine) and *move time* (the actual movement to the next machine, finished goods inventory, or the end customer).

Time Phasing/Lead-Time Offsetting—Time phasing enables you to look into the future in order to plan.

This lead-time offset is established by determining when the part is needed to satisfy a requirement. This allows the MRP system to schedule a planned order receipt in one time period and the planned order release in an earlier time period. The difference between these two dates is the required lead time to make or buy.

DETERMINE GROSS-TO-NET REQUIREMENTS (continued)

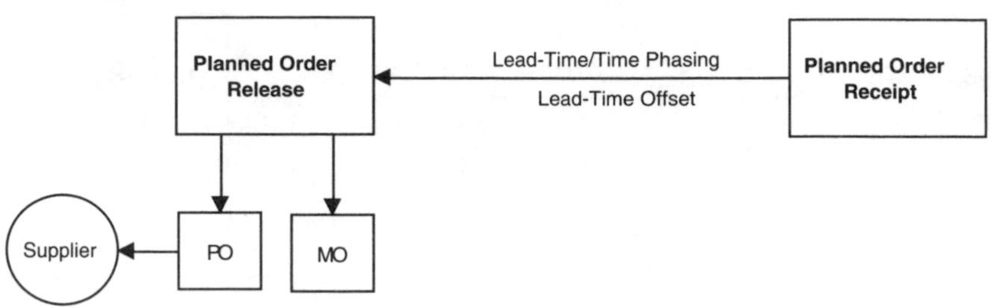

Planned Order Release—A planned order release suggests an order be created, including quantity, release date, and due date. It suggests that a purchase order (PO) or manufacturing order (MO) is to be created. Planned orders exist only within the MRP system and may be changed or deleted by the computer during subsequent MRP processing if conditions change.

The planned order release results in purchase orders, which are given to suppliers, and manufacturing orders, which are sent to the shop floor. In the case of an MO, a planned order release at one level creates a gross requirement at the next level.

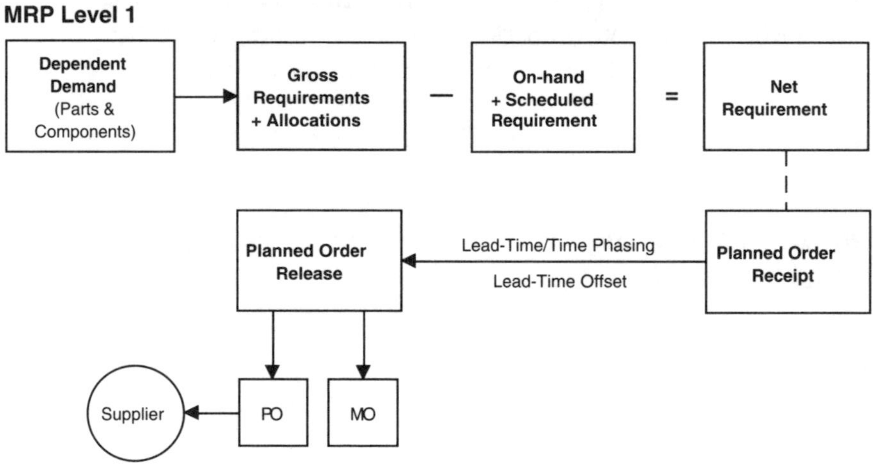

Dependent Demand—Dependent Demand is the demand for all the components required to satisfy the dependent or independent demand from a higher level.

Dependent demand is directly related to or derived from the BOM structure for other components or end products. These demands are calculated, not forecasted. Independent demand is forecasted, and any given item may have both dependent and independent demand. For example, a part may be the component of an assembly, and also be sold as a service part. The MRP represents dependent demand.

RELEASING MOs TO THE SHOP FLOOR

When you open an MO, you release it to the manufacturing floor. An MO is a document, group of documents, or schedule conveying authority for the manufacture of specified parts or products in specified quantities.

Routing

The document that describes where on the shop floor the material needs to be sent is called a "routing."

A routing is a set of information detailing the method of manufacture of a particular item. It includes the operations to be performed, their sequence, the various work centers to be involved and the standards for setup and run. In some companies, the routing also includes information on tooling, operator skill levels, inspection operations and testing requirements.

RELEASING MOs TO THE SHOP FLOOR (continued)

Summary

You have completed the material control phase of the short-term planning process. The output of the material control phase is the material requirements plan. In the next module, production activity control, you will learn about capacity requirements planning, which uses the MRP output of scheduled receipts as well as planned orders.

The portion of the manufacturing formula and the related tools and techniques applicable to this module are highlighted as follows:

Basic Manufacturing Formula	**Units**	**Dollars**	**Tools/Techniques**
Beginning Inventory	1,000	1,000	From last year's audited financial statement
+ Production (Build Plan)	9,500	9,500	• Resource Requirement Plan • Rated Capacity calculation • Just-in-Time (JIT) manufacturing • Material requirement planning (MRP)
= Available Inventory to Ship	10,500	10,500	
– Shipments/Sales	10,000	10,000	• Customer orders (lead-time management) • Forecast: —Forecast error —Customer service level/probability
= Ending Inventory	500	500	• ABC/Classification

Module 4 Exercise

1. List what you know about product F. The answers are on pages 109–110 in the back of the book.

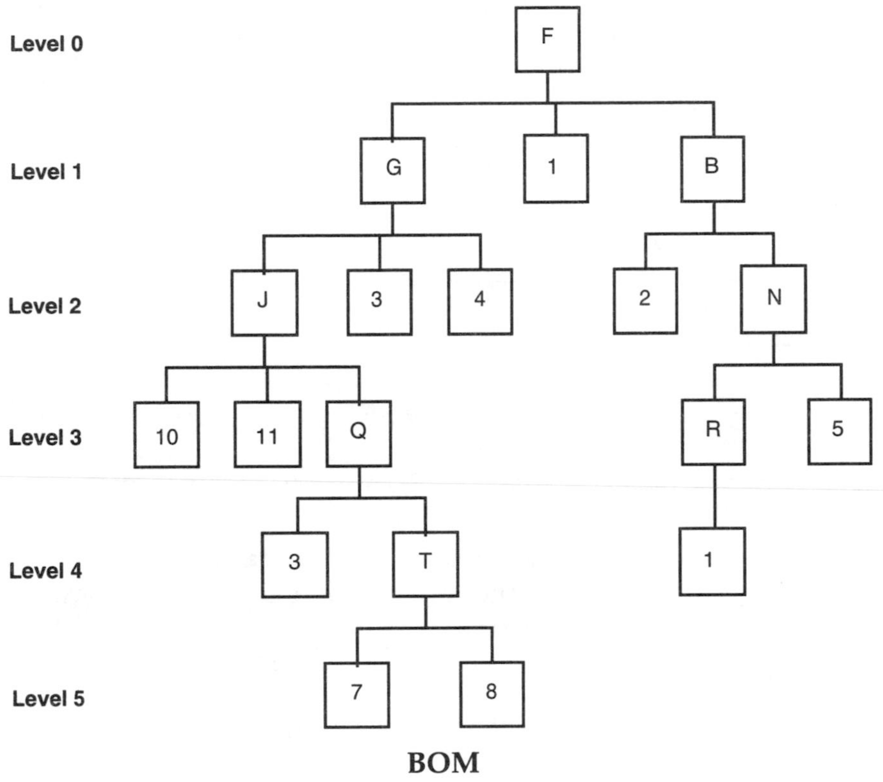

BOM

a. ____

b. ____

c. ____

d. ____

e. ____

f. ____

MODULE 4 EXERCISE (continued)

2. What do you know about levels below product F? List at least five.

a. ______

b. ______

c. ______

d. ______

e. ______

f. ______

g. ______

h. ______

3. In this exercise you will build on what you've learned by doing a complete MRP calculation for product F. For the following situations, determine the planned order releases.

Lead-time: **3 weeks** Lot size: **250**

What would be the balance at the end of the day for Period 1? What is the beginning inventory for Period 2?

Planning period = 9 periods

	Period								
	1	**2**	**3**	**4**	**5**	**6**	**7**	**8**	**9**
Gross Requirements	150	100	200	50	150	250	100	150	200
Scheduled Receipts	250								
Projected On Hand = 250									
Net Requirements									
Planned Order Receipts									
Planned Order Release									

4. What are key words that can be used to define the following terms?

a. ______________________ is a priority-setting process that attempts to schedule the right part, at the right time, in the right place.

b. ______________________ is the demand for an end item or service part that is unrelated to the demand for other items. It is created from such sources as customer orders for end products and spare parts, the forecast and intercompany orders.

c. ______________________ is the demand for parts that are included in the bill of material.

d. ______________________ is the total demand from independent demand and dependent demand.

e. ______________________ is an order that is planned to be received in the future.

f. ______________________ is an order that is planned to be released in the future.

g. ______________________ occurs when the gross requirements exceed the projected on-hand balance and scheduled receipt for a certain time period.

5. Why establish a parent/component relationship?

____

____

____

____

____

____

M O D U L E

V

Short-Term Planning Phase II: Production Activity Control

Learning Objectives

After completing this module, you will be able to:

- Define the major components of production activity control
- Describe the different types of manufacturing environments

PRODUCTION ACTIVITY CONTROL

The second phase of short-term planning is production activity control. Figure 5-1 illustrates the specific activities involved in all three short-term planning phases.

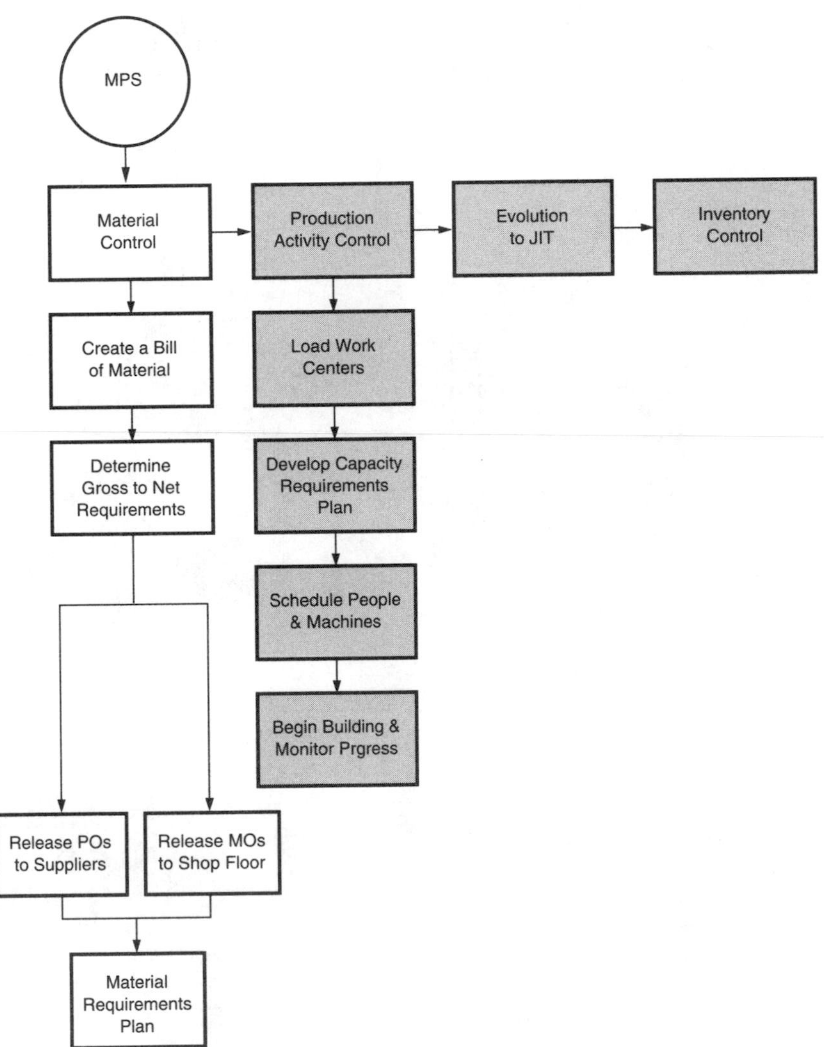

Figure 5-1: Short-Term Planning

PRODUCTION ACTIVITY CONTROL (continued)

The production process is the conversion of materials by direct labor into parts, subassemblies, assemblies, and finally the end item for the customer.

To complete the work on schedule, the suppliers must meet their deadlines and all of the work centers must finish their work on time.

DEFINE PRODUCTION ACTIVITY CONTROL

Key Question

How is capacity determined in a build-to-order manufacturing environment

Production activity control (PAC) involves the scheduling and rescheduling of people and/or machines to put together the components that eventually make up the products that are shipped to customers.

Production activity control, also known as shop-floor control, is used primarily in two types of manufacturing environments. The first is manufacturing environments that are predominantly **build-to-customer specification,** or to-engineering specification. These environments tend to be characterized by great product variety and low volumes. As a result, the emphasis is on the progression of specific customer orders through the shop floor via the fastest method possible. Since customer orders are already in hand, however, there is a little more flexibility in allowing orders to be released to the shop floor earlier than actually needed.

Production activity control or shop floor planning also is used in manufacturing environments that are more traditional—where there is more inventory than needed. The traditional environments typically exist in companies that build to stock or assemble to order. The **build-to-stock** environment is characterized by a high level of finished goods in inventory. An **assemble-to-order** environment is characterized by higher levels of work in process waiting for final assembly once the customers' orders are received. Frequently, produced inventory sat at the next work station or in the warehouse waiting for a customer. Many of these environments are changing to just-in-time (JIT) practice. An expanded discussion of this evolution toward JIT is provided in the next module.

In both traditional and JIT manufacturing environments, batches of material are released in predetermined quantities (lot sizes) by MRP. They move through a predetermined sequence of steps in the production process, eventually ending up as shippable products.

In the build-to-customer order environment, the production process is affected by the capacity of each work station (a machine and/or person) and the load of planned and released manufacturing orders.

DEFINE PRODUCTION ACTIVITY CONTROL (continued)

Determining the capacity of each work station is part of the detailed capacity requirements planning process. **Capacity requirements planning** also involves scheduling people and machines to work on the material that has been released by the materials requirement planning system.

Capacity of any machine and/or person equals output. Output is estimated by the rated capacity calculation using this formula:

> hours per shift × the number of shifts per day × the number of machines and/or people × utilization × efficiency = hours of capacity per day × units per hour = units per day of capacity.

The use of this formula tells you the hours of machine and/or people capacity available to complete manufacturing orders. You can convert the output in hours to units of output by dividing the output in hours by predetermined engineering estimates of units produced per hour.

A **work center** is a grouping of one or many machines and/or people performing tasks called out by a *routing*. In addition to indicating the sequence of machines and/or people required to produce the part, the routing also details the work to be performed at each machine (work center), tooling required, skill levels, and any testing required.

LOAD WORK CENTERS

Loading Orders

The **loading** of orders at each work center is accomplished through back scheduling. **Back scheduling** establishes the operation start and completion dates for each step in the process required to complete the order. To back schedule, you start with the ship date for the order and work backward to determine the required start date and/or completion dates for each operation. You begin with the order due date and offset the lead time through each work center specified in the routing.

Forward Scheduling

Forward scheduling identifies the earliest date by which material is received from the supplier and released to the shop floor in the sequence specified by the routing. Because of the computed resources required, this type of scheduling is not often used.

Input/Output Control

The result of forward and backward scheduling through the routing sequence is an input/output report for each work center that shows planned input; planned output; and planned backlog, load and work in process (WIP).

Input/Output Control is a technique for capacity control in which you can monitor planned and actual inputs and planned and actual outputs of a work center. Planned inputs and outputs for each work center are developed by capacity requirements planning and approved by manufacturing management. Actual input is compared to planned input to identify when a work center's output might vary from the plan because work is not available at the work center. Actual output is also compared to planned output to identify problems within the work center.

Figure 5-2 on page 68 shows an example of an Input/Output Control Chart.

LOAD WORK CENTERS (continued)

Work Center 601 (all figures in standard hours)

Week	11	12	13	14	15	16
Planned Input	50	50	50	50	50	50
Actual Input	0	100	0	50	55	35
Cumulative Deviation	–50	0	–50	–50	–45	60

Week	11	12	13	14	15	16
Planned Output	60	60	60	60	60	60
Actual Output	45	70	40	50	45	50
Cumulative Deviation	–15	–5	–25	–35	–50	–60
Work-in-progress (WIP) Inventory 100	55	85	45	45	55	40

Note: Backlog at the beginning of Week 11 was 100 standard hours. The WIP during each subsequent week is based on actual input and output.

Figure 5-2: Input/Output Control Chart

The result of detailed capacity requirement planning and loading of planned and released orders is a **load profile.** A load profile is a bar graph (such as that in Figure 5-3) that shows the released and planned orders scheduled for any given work day.

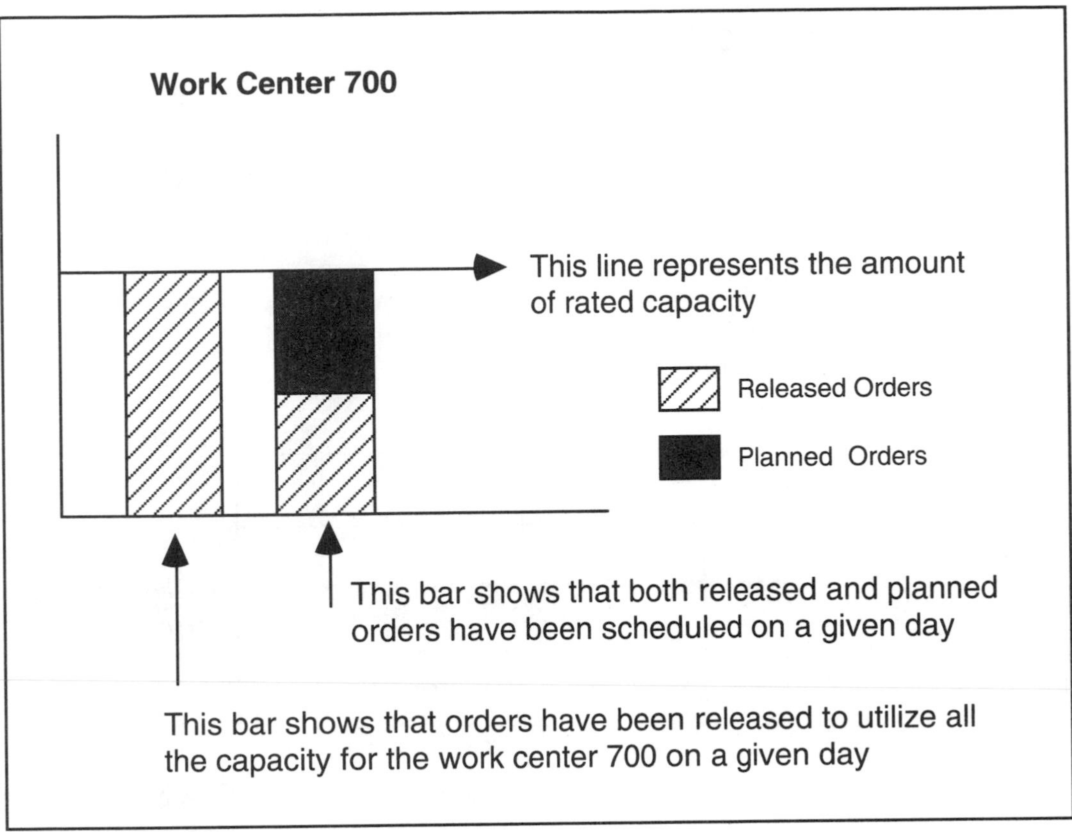

Figure 5-3: Load Profile

Infinite Loading

Some companies use a process called "infinite and finite loading." **Infinite loading** is the loading of manufacturing orders required at work centers in the time periods required. Infinite loading assumes that you have unlimited capacity. Figure 5-4 is an example of infinite loading.

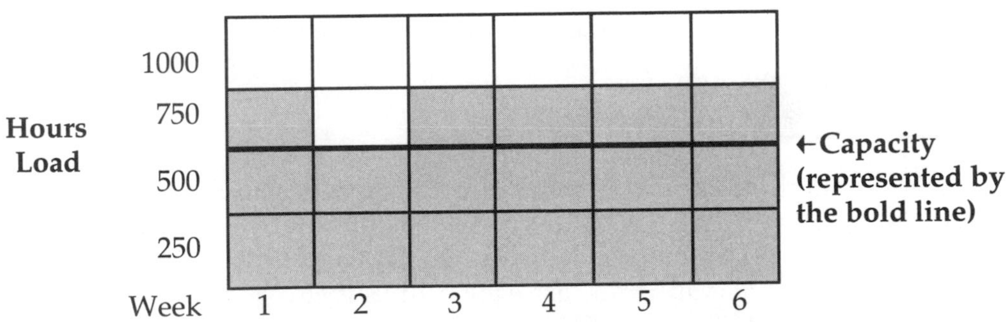

Figure 5-4: Infinite Loading (gray areas represent orders)

LOAD WORK CENTERS (continued)

Finite Loading

Finite loading is the activity of assigning no more work to a work center than that center can be expected to complete in a given time period. The specific term usually refers to a computer technique that calculates shop priority revisions in order to level load operation by operation. The following is an example of finite loading.

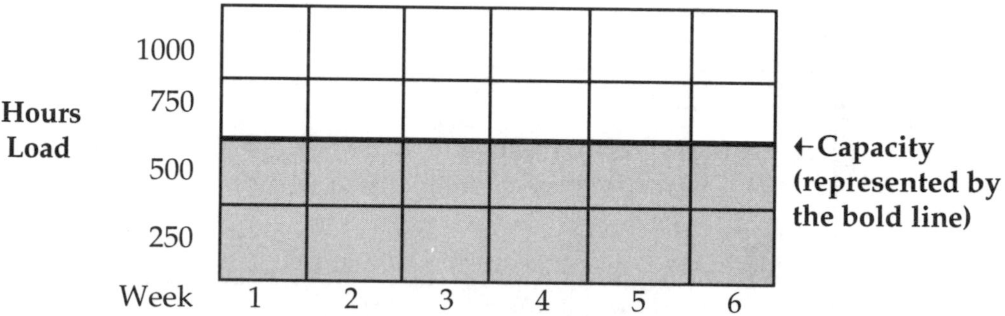

Figure 5-5: Finite Loading (gray areas represent orders)

Dispatch List

When a work center has been loaded with more than one day's supply of material related to orders, a dispatch list is created that sets the priority of manufacturing orders to be worked on (first, second, third, etc.).

The dispatch list contains detailed information on priority, location, quantity, and the capacity requirements of the manufacturing order by operation. Dispatch lists are normally generated daily for each work center.

Product Mix

To this point, all orders have been based on a forecasted or actual product mix. The product mix is the proportion of individual products that make up the total production and/or sales volume. Changes in the product mix can mean drastic changes in manufacturing requirements for certain types of labor and material. Changes in the product mix must be entered into the MRP system and then the system is updated.

BEGIN BUILDING AND MONITORING PROGRESS

When all the orders have been loaded and the product is being built, you must constantly monitor the progress of each order through the production floor. Inevitably, changes in customer priorities, the inability of suppliers to meet their commitments and unforeseen problems on the shop floor will require adjustments to be made to capacity or load.

Capacity can be increased by scheduling overtime, adding shifts, or adding people and equipment. Conversely, capacity can be decreased by reducing the length of shifts, eliminating shifts, or layoffs.

Load can be increased by manufacturing items internally that are normally purchased or subcontracted. Load also can be increased by releasing orders early or increasing lot sizes. Load can be reduced by decreasing lot sizes, holding work in production control, or subcontracting work externally.

The second type of production covered in this book involves production in a just-in-time environment, the topic of the next module.

BEGIN BUILDING AND MONITORING PROGRESS (continued)

Summary

This module discussed the activities involved in production activity control, including: loading work centers, determining capacity, beginning building and monitoring progress. The primary tool covered in this module is highlighted as follows.

Basic Manufacturing Formula	**Units**	**Dollars**	**Tools/Techniques**
Beginning Inventory	1,000	1,000	From last year's audited financial statement
+ Production (Build Plan)	9,500	9,500	• Resource Requirement Plan • Rated Capacity calculation • Just-in-Time (JIT) manufacturing • Material requirement planning (MRP)
= Available Inventory to Ship	10,500	10,500	
– Shipments/Sales	10,000	10,000	• Customer orders (lead-time management) • Forecast: —Forecast error —Customer service level/probability
= Ending Inventory	500	500	• ABC/Classification

Module 5 Exercise

Answer the following questions true or false. The answers are on page 111 in the back of the book.

_____ **1.** The output of any machine and/or person is the capacity.

_____ **2.** The process of establishing the latest operation start and completion dates for each step in the process required to complete an order is the load profile.

_____ **3.** Assemble-to-order is an environment characterized by low product variety and high volume.

_____ **4.** The activity of assigning no more work to a work center than the center can be expected to execute in a given period of time is the production activity control.

_____ **5.** Infinite loading assumes infinite capacity.

_____ **6.** A technique for capacity control in which planned and actual inputs and outputs of a work center are monitored is the capacity requirements planning.

_____ **7.** Back scheduling is the process of establishing operation start and completion dates for each step in the process required to complete an order.

_____ **8.** Finite capacity planning is the activity of assigning no more work to a work center than it can be expected to execute in a given time.

_____ **9.** Production activity control is a short-term planning process that is used in build-to-order and traditional manufacturing environments.

_____ **10.** A load profile is the loading of manufacturing orders required at work centers in the time periods required.

MODULE 5 EXERCISE (continued)

_____ **11.** Build-to-stock is an environment characterized by low product variety and high volume.

_____ **12.** Capacity requirements planning is the major component of production activity control.

_____ **13.** In a build-to-custom order, the emphasis is on moving the orders through as fast as possible.

_____ **14.** A grouping of one or more machines and/or people performing tasks called out by a routing is called a load.

_____ **15.** In manufacturing, batches of material are released in lot sizes predetermined by MRP.

M O D U L E

VI

Short-Term Planning Phase III: Evolution to JIT Manufacturing

Learning Objectives

After completing this module, you will be able to:

- Explain how a pull system differs from the traditional system
- List the steps required to evolve to a pull system from a push system

JUST-IN-TIME MANUFACTURING

Just-in-time (JIT) manufacturing evolved from work done in the area of quality control from the early 1950s through the 1980s. JIT programs were influenced by continuous process improvements. From a broad view, just-in-time is a philosophy. From a very narrow view, just-in-time means scheduling the right part, at the right place, at the right time.

Total quality control and total quality management have been the driving forces behind the evolution toward JIT.

Figure 6-1 shows this third phase of the overall short-term planning process.

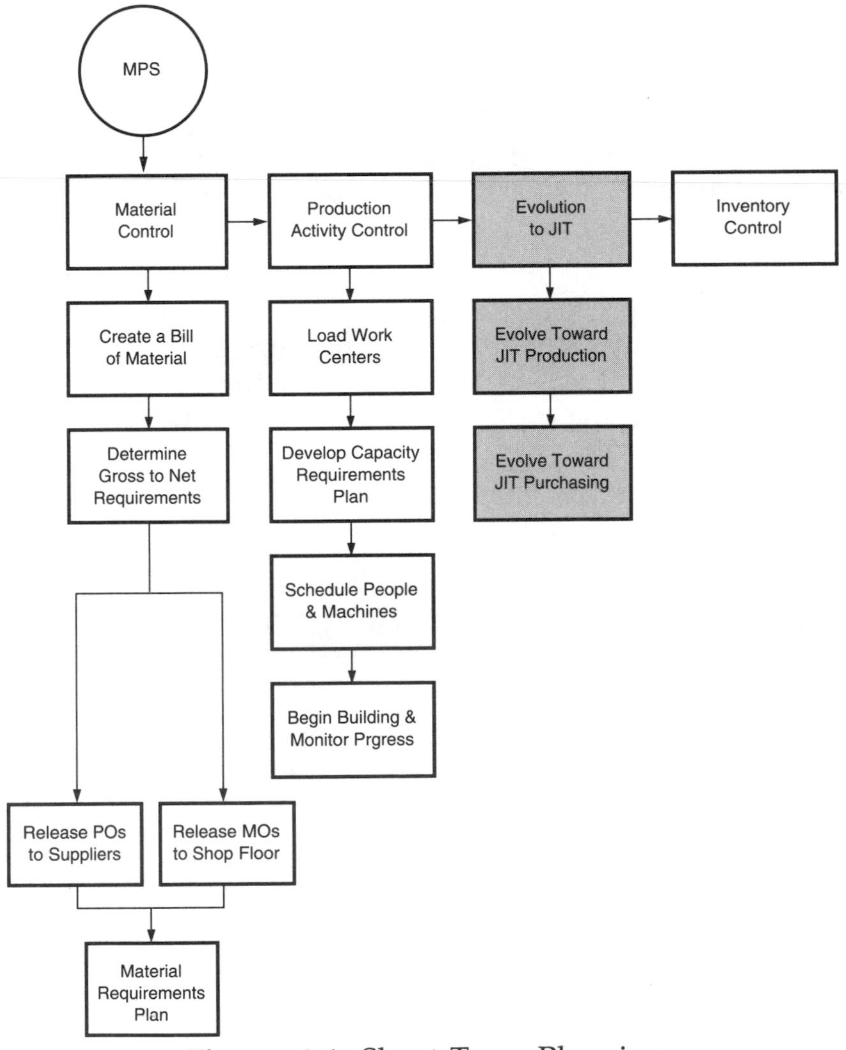

Figure 6-1: Short-Term Planning

IMPLEMENT JIT PRINCIPLES

Key Question

How does a traditional production environment evolve toward a Just-in-Time environment

There are three major areas in which JIT principles can be implemented:

1. **Production and Manufacturing**

   Most companies begin with JIT production by building *X* units per day per week in a linear fashion to meet the monthly demand.

2. **Purchasing and Supplier Management**

   Next, companies focus on getting suppliers to deliver materials needed for building assemblies and subassemblies.

3. **Shipments and Forecasting**

   The final area of focus is shipments. Most companies never focus on forecasting more accurately. JIT manufacturing theory assumes that, as customers place orders, these orders are shipped only when needed. If demand fluctuates, however, there must be inventory to buffer this fluctuation. This means that fluctuation must be forecasted.

Achieve JIT Objectives

To understand the evolution to JIT and how JIT objectives are achieved, start with the traditional batch production environment. Figure 6-2 on page 79 shows the typical MRP system. This production environment was described in the previous module. The master production schedule drives the MRP. In this modified example, end item F is made up of part B and part 3. Part B is made up of 1 and 2.

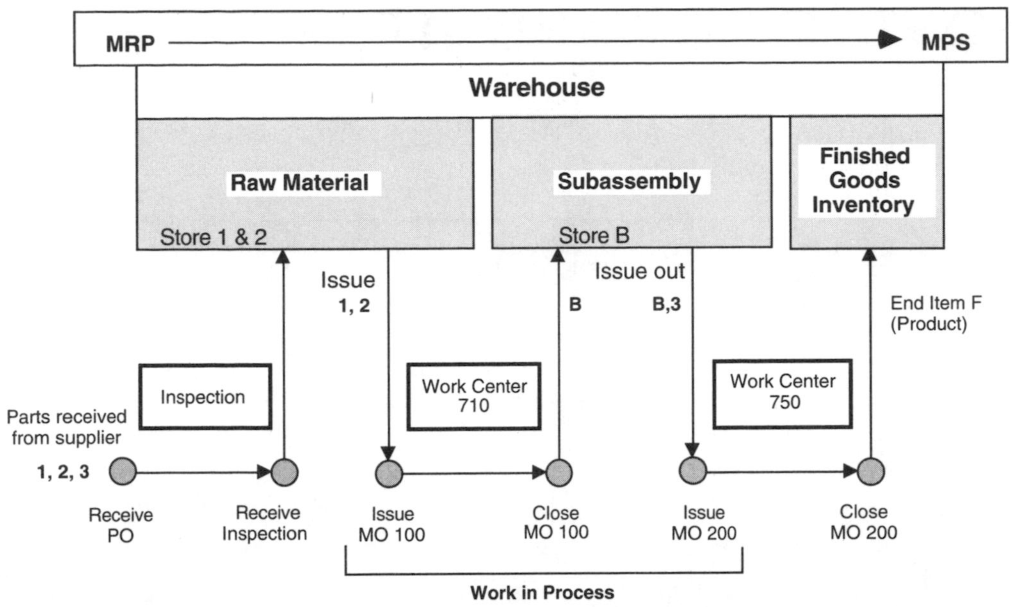

Figure 6-2: Traditional Batch Production

Figure 6-3 shows the simple BOM for end item F. Parts 1, 2, and 3 would be delivered by the supplier, received into inspection and, if accepted, would move into the warehouse to be stored. At the appropriate time, MRP would release the parts as manufacturing orders to a work center. In this example parts 1 and 2 are released to work center number 710, where they are assembled. Here, direct labor is added. When the manufacturing order is completed, overhead is allocated.

Once the manufacturing order (#100) is completed, it is closed and subassembly B is moved back into the warehouse, where it sits again, until such time as item 3 comes in from the supplier. Now parts 1 and 2—which have become B—are issued out as B to work center 750, where B is combined with 3 to make up an F. The combining of B and 3 through the use of direct labor creates F. (Overhead is again added at this level.) This process of adding material, labor, and overhead cost at each level results in the final cost of the product.

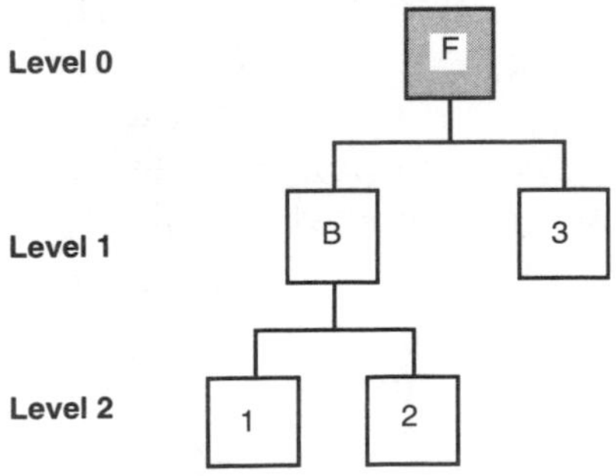

Figure 6-3: Simple BOM

MOVING TOWARD JIT

The movement from the traditional production environment toward a JIT production environment is accomplished by:

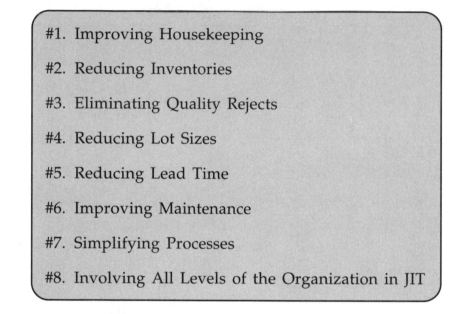

#1. Improving Housekeeping

#2. Reducing Inventories

#3. Eliminating Quality Rejects

#4. Reducing Lot Sizes

#5. Reducing Lead Time

#6. Improving Maintenance

#7. Simplifying Processes

#8. Involving All Levels of the Organization in JIT

How to Begin

To evolve from the traditional production environment, characterized by waste, to a JIT production environment, the first place to start is housekeeping.

#1. Improving Housekeeping

Housekeeping means removing all items that are not really essential to performing the operation or the job. Examples include excess parts, personal items, tools that are not being used, and defective material—all of those get cleaned up. The first step, then, is to clean up the work area, organize the shop, and define who is responsible for keeping that work area clean. The result is better organization and improved visibility.

#2. Reducing Inventories

By moving excess inventory—more than can be used in a 24-hour period—off the shop floor and back into the warehouse, the overall work-in-progress inventory is reduced. Total inventory can be further reduced by using up this excess before placing additional orders. This inventory reduction also reduces lead time and contributes to faster time-to-market. Physical inventories are faster, easier, and more accurate.

#3. Eliminating Quality Rejects

Elimination of inspection, from incoming inspection to elimination of all inspection throughout the production process, is an important part of the evolution toward JIT production. Inspection adds no value to the product; indeed, it increases lead-time. Inventory should be continuously reduced by releasing only the amount of inventory to the shop floor to satisfy demand.

#4. Reducing Lot Sizes

Lot size quantities should be reduced and released to the production floor only when needed. Queues are reduced, thus reducing the overall manufacturing lead-time.

#5. Reducing Lead Time

The reduction in overall manufacturing lead-time in turn allows for faster deliveries to customers. The reduction in work-in-process inventory allows work centers eventually to move closer together, thus reducing the time required to move inventory.

The reduction in move time adds to the overall reduction total manufacturing lead-time. Set-up times can be reduced by simplifying the machine set-up procedures, ensuring accurate documentation of how to set up and reducing the amount of scrapped product turned out during set up. This reduction in set-up time reduces the lead-time and increases the use of the machine, thus increasing its capacity.

MOVING TOWARD JIT (continued)

#6. Improving Maintenance

Improved machine maintenance and the subsequent reduction in unplanned down time also reduces lead-times and contributes to the JIT production environment.

All of these reductions in waste save money, improve customer satisfaction (because deliveries are faster) and lead to more effective use of machinery and equipment.

#7. Simplifying Processes

Once processes are documented, waste such as excess inventory, effort, etc., can be eliminated. This elimination of waste simplifies the process, which in turn allows the product to flow through these processes faster.

#8. Involving All Levels of the Organization in JIT

For the types of changes that have been discussed to take place, all functional groups must be involved. JIT is an organization-wide concept, not just a manufacturing responsibility.

SWITCHING TO A "DEMAND PULL" SYSTEM

The JIT production environment is described many times as a demand pull versus the demand push system used in the more traditional production environment. The demand push system puts more inventory on the shop floor than can be used in the manufacturing process in twenty-four hours. A **demand pull** system is essentially a visual feedback control system, both within and between work centers, ending with final assembly of the end item to satisfy the customers' demands.

Figure 6-4 illustrates a JIT system in which the improvements described previously have been made (for example, elimination of inspection and reductions in inventory).

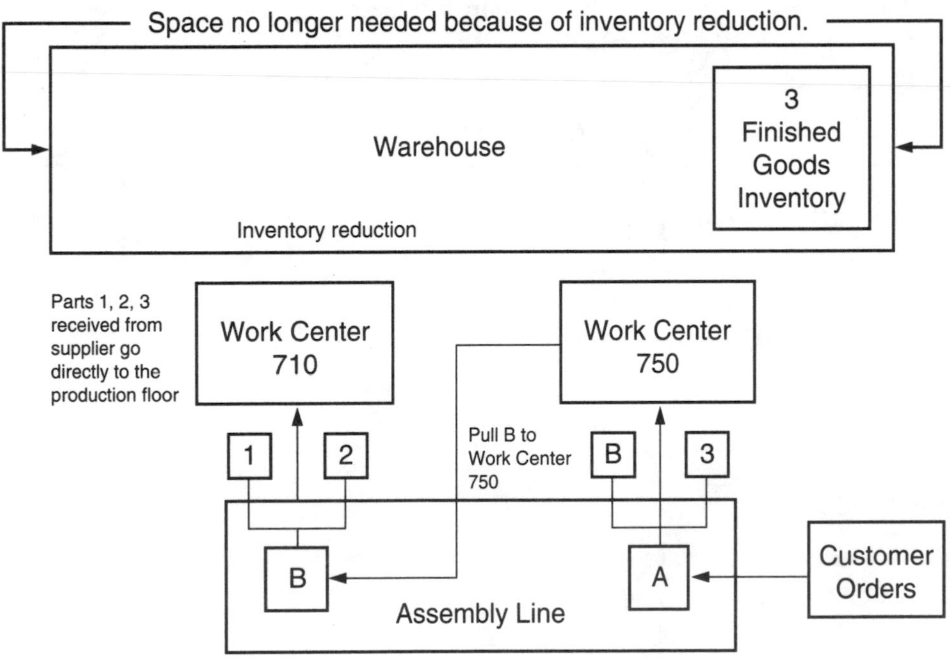

Figure 6-4: Demand Pull System

This figure shows that are you no longer receiving the parts 1, 2 and 3 from the warehouse, but in fact are bypassing the warehouse and going directly to work center 710. Parts 1 and 2 are put together to become B, then B is pulled to work center 750, where the supplier has delivered component 3. Parts 3 and B are combined to make part A, which is then pulled from finished goods and delivered to the customer. This is a very simplistic description of how you evolve from a traditional push system to what is characterized as a pull system.

SWITCHING TO A "DEMAND PULL" SYSTEM (continued)

The results of JIT or a combination of quality programs and JIT are that inventory decreases, quality continues to improve, lot sizes are reduced, lead-times go down, preventive maintenance ordinarily improves, and processes overall become simpler. As a result, you realize significant reduction in inventory and the cost of carrying this inventory.

Mechanics of a Pull System

The mechanics of JIT production involve recording the accounting impact of physical flow to reconcile the physical transactions with the book transactions. Reconciling the physical flow with the accounting records must be done at least monthly so the books can be closed. Some companies do this bimonthly or weekly. Figure 6-5 illustrates a physical flow.

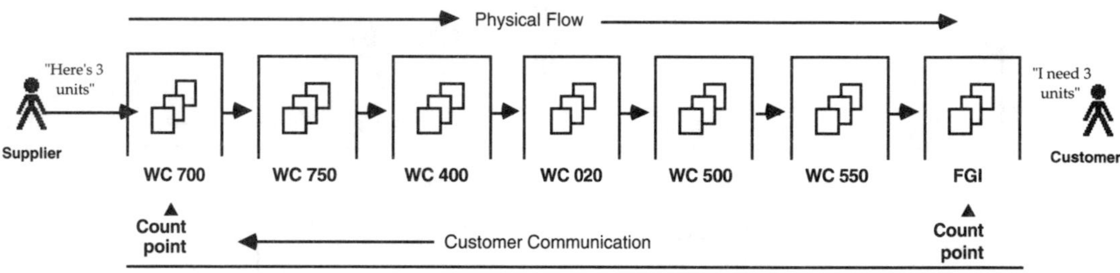

Figure 6-5: Physical Flow

Rate and Mix:

Rate is the overall rate at which all units are being produced. Mix is the proportion of models, options and various materials requested within the overall rate.

Count Point:

Count point is a point in the physical manufacturing process at which counts are taken of the parts, subassemblies, and end items. Count points can be anywhere along the production line, however there must be one at the end of the line to record the demand. Count points enable the accounting transactions to be updated at least monthly.

Count Point Backflush:

This is a technique that explodes back through the bill of material to account for the material, labor and overhead for an end item. Adjustments for things such as scrap, rework and extra usage must be entered into the system to reconcile the book records and the accounting records. In a two-card system, move cards and production cards are used.

Move Card *(or other signal):*

A move card indicates the number of parts, sub-assemblies and so forth that are to move from one point in the production process to the next. This card gives authority to move a part between work centers. Information on move cards includes the using and supplying of a work center, capacity part numbers, and so on. Kanban (signal) is a signaling technique used in a pull environment to indicate a withdrawal of parts from feeding operations or suppliers.

Production Card:

A production card indicates the quantity and the part number to be produced, the materials and their location, the card number, the supplying work center number, other information such as tooling and location of materials, and so on.

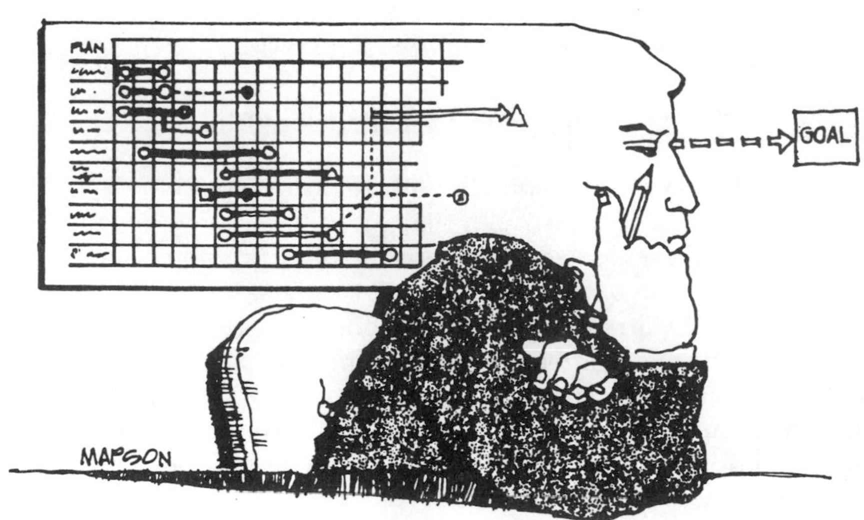

EDUCATING YOUR SUPPLIERS

Key Question

How do you get suppliers to produce only what you need

Once your organization is far enough along in the JIT production process, you can begin to educate your suppliers as to what new requirements you will expect from them as JIT suppliers.

Selecting Suppliers

As a preliminary step, you reduce the number of suppliers providing the same part. This selection process is based on the following characteristics of a good supplier:

- Delivers on time in the right quantity
- Supplies parts that require no incoming inspection
- Sets fair prices and terms
- Cooperates to solve problems

A "bad" supplier exhibits these characteristics:

- Delivers late or early and in the wrong quantity
- Supplies parts that require incoming inspection
- Sets terms that are unacceptable with regard to price
- Indicates unwillingness to cooperate to solve problems

The selection process will result in your working with fewer suppliers. In some situations, you might find yourself working with only one supplier, who gets 100 percent of the business. This single-source supplier should be backed up with at least one alternative supplier who can build the same part. You may want to split the demand for a product and give a certain percentage to another supplier. Single-sourcing is different from sole-sourcing, in that a sole source is the only company that produces the product.

Summary

This module has discussed the steps involved in transitioning from a traditional production environment to just-in-time environment. You learned that just-in-time principles can be implemented in three areas: production/manufacturing, purchasing/supplier management, and shipments/forecasting.

The primary tool discussed in this module is highlighted as follows.

Basic Manufacturing Formula	Units	Dollars	Tools/Techniques
Beginning Inventory	1,000	1,000	From last year's audited financial statement
+ Production (Build Plan)	9,500	9,500	• Resource Requirement Plan • Rated Capacity calculation • Just-in-Time (JIT) manufacturing • Material requirement planning (MRP)
= Available Inventory to Ship	10,500	10,500	
– Shipments/Sales	10,000	10,000	• Customer orders (lead-time management) • Forecast: —Forecast error —Customer service level/probability
= Ending Inventory	500	500	• ABC/Classification

Module 6 Exercise

1. The traditional production environment results in tremendous waste. List at least five examples of waste in the "traditional" production environment. The answers are on pages 111–112 in the back of the book.

2. How are JIT goals achieved?

3. What are four characteristics of a good supplier?

4. Define the following terms.

a. *Demand pull:* ____________________

____

b. *Backflush:* ____________________

____

c. *Count point:* ____________________

____

d. *Production card:* ____________________

____

e. *Move card:* ____________________

____

M O D U L E

VII

Short-Term Planning Phase IV: Inventory Control

Learning Objectives

After completing this module, you will be able to:

- Explain the importance of inventory management
- Explain the difference between the push system and the pull systems in a distribution environment

INVENTORY CONTROL

This module focuses on the fourth and final phase of short-term planning: Inventory Control. Figure 7-1 illustrates the specific activities involved in each phase of the short-term planning process.

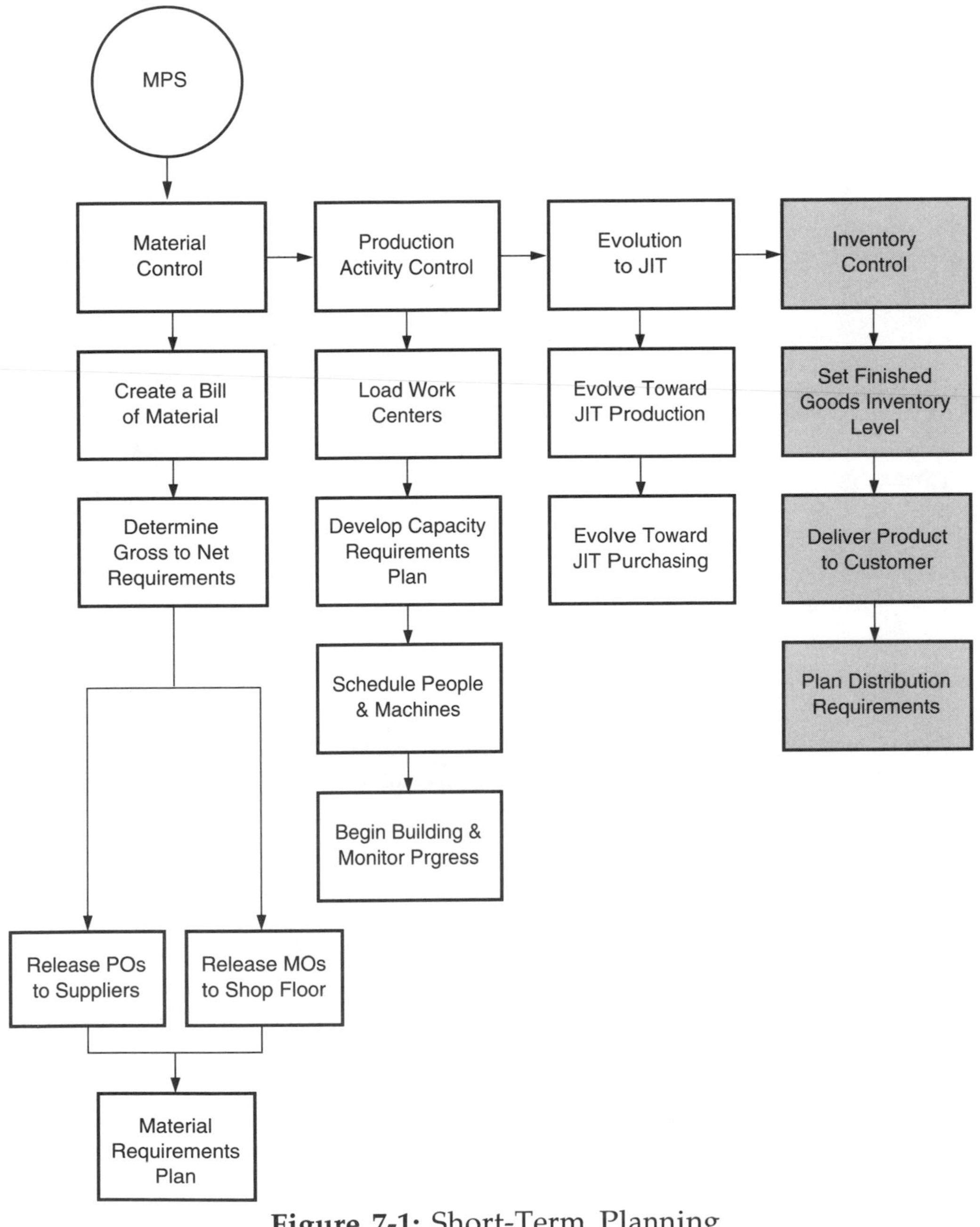

Figure 7-1: Short-Term Planning

SET FINISHED GOODS INVENTORY LEVEL

Key Question

How much inventory do you need to buffer against fluctuations in the forecast and customer demand 

What Is Inventory Management?

The objective of inventory management is to replace a very expensive asset called "inventory" with a less expensive asset called "information." In order to accomplish this objective, the information must be timely, accurate, reliable and consistent.

Why Manage Inventory?

You manage inventory to:

- Minimize inventory investment
- Maximize customer service
- Maximize efficiency of people and machines
- Maximize profit

What Are the Inventory Categories?

There are three major categories of inventory:

- **Direct material/warehouse stock:** Material that becomes a part of the final product
- **Work in process (WIP):** A product or products in various stages of completion throughout the plant
- **Finished goods:** Products that are available for sale

Physical and Financial Inventory Control

Inventory must be controlled both physically and financially. **Physical inventory control** is accomplished by restricting access to the inventory and counting what is physically on hand. Physical inventories can be taken on a continuous or periodic basis. Most companies today control inventory by updating the physical activity so that the status of the physical inventory on hand can be reconciled to the accounting records at any time. This reconciliation with accounting records results in **financial control over inventory.**

Periodically, most companies take a physical inventory, which may be a complete wall-to-wall inventory, and/or a cycle count of the inventory. Because of legal requirements, all companies take a physical inventory.

Cycle Counting

Cycle counting is a common way of controlling physical inventory. It is usually done on a regular basis (often more frequently for high-value or fast-moving items and less frequently for low-value or slow-moving items). Most effective cycle-counting systems require the counting of a certain number of items every workday, with each item counted at a prescribed frequency.

The purpose of cycle counting is to identify errors and correct conditions causing the errors. Cycle counting allows you to report an accurate statement of inventory on the balance sheet. When inventory records are consistently accurate, less inventory is necessary.

ABC CLASSIFICATION

Most cycle-counting systems determine the frequency of counting parts based on the value of usage. An **ABC classification system** is used. This system groups items in decreasing order of annual dollar volume (price × projected volume). Items are normally split into three categories, called A, B and C.

A Items have the highest value. These are relatively few items (15–20 percent) whose value accounts for 75–80 percent of the total value of the inventory. As a general rule, 20 percent of the items constitute 80 percent of the annual requirements.

B Items have medium value. These are a larger number in the middle of the list, usually about 30–40 percent of the items, whose value accounts for about 15 percent of the total.

C Items have low value. These are the bulk of the items, usually about 40–50 percent, whose total inventory value is almost negligible, accounting for only 5–10 percent of the value.

ABC Analysis Calculation Steps

1. Calculate annual usage in units for each item.
2. Multiply usage by unit cost to determine annual dollar usage.
3. Rank annual dollar usage from highest to lowest.
4. Assign ABC categories.

DELIVER PRODUCT TO THE CUSTOMER

Key Question

What is Involved in Distribution Planning 

Distribution Logistics

Logistics includes the activities of acquiring material (procurement), moving material through manufacturing (production and inventory) and distribution (getting the products to, or close to, the final customer). This module focuses on the distribution portion of logistics.

Distribution involves meeting customer requirements. However, you also want to receive and store material at the least possible cost, as well as meet customer requirements both internally and externally. In most cases, distribution begins with entry of the customer's order and ends with delivery of the product to the customer.

Distribution resource planning (DRP) extends distribution requirements planning into the planning of key resources contained in a distribution system: warehouse space, work force, money, trucks, freight cars and so on.

In distribution systems that replenish field warehouse inventories, replenishment decisions are made at the field warehouse itself, not at the central warehouse or plant.

Types of Distribution Systems

Distribution systems are loosely classified as either a push or a pull system. A **push system** pushes the inventory from a central factory out to the warehouse. Replenishment decisions are made at the manufacturing site. DRP is the most widely used push system.

DELIVER PRODUCT TO THE CUSTOMER (continued)

Distribution Requirements Planning (DRP)

To determine what is needed at a branch warehouse, DRP uses a time-phased order point approach. In DRP the planned orders at the branch warehouse are "exploded" via MRP logic to become gross requirements for the various levels of regional warehouses, factory warehouses, and so on, and then becomes input to the master production schedule.

Order Point

This is a pull system. Order point sets an inventory level at which, if the total stock on hand plus on order falls to or below that point, action is taken to replenish the stock. The order point is normally calculated as forecasted usage during the replenishment lead time, plus safety stock. The order point system is an inventory method that places an order for a lot whenever the quantity on hand is reduced to a predetermined level known as the order point.

Double Order Point System

Another distribution inventory management system has two order points. The smallest equals the original order point, which covers replenishment lead-time. The second order point is the sum of the first order point plus normal usage during manufacturing lead-time. This system enables warehouses to forewarn manufacturing of future replenishment orders.

Stock Keeping Unit (SKU)

Stock keeping units (SKUs) are items located at a particular geographic location. For example, one product stocked at the plant and at six different distribution centers, would represent seven SKUs.

Summary

This module has discussed activities in inventory control, the final phase of the short-term planning process. You learned how to set the finished goods inventory level, and what is involved in delivering the product to the customer. The specific tool covered in this module is highlighted as follows.

Basic Manufacturing Formula	Units	Dollars	Tools/Techniques
Beginning Inventory	1,000	1,000	From last year's audited financial statement
+ Production (Build Plan)	9,500	9,500	• Resource Requirement Plan • Rated Capacity calculation • Just-in-Time (JIT) manufacturing • Material requirement planning (MRP)
= Available Inventory to Ship	10,500	10,500	
– Shipments/Sales	10,000	10,000	• Customer orders (lead-time management) • Forecast: —Forecast error —Customer service level/probability
= Ending Inventory	500	500	• ABC/Classification

Module 7 Exercise

1. In this exercise you will use an ABC classification analysis. First, multiply column 1 by column 2 to determine the annual usage in dollars. Then calculate percentage of total dollar usage. The answers are on pages 113–115 in the back of the book.

ABC Analysis Based on Annual Dollar Volume

A. Annual Dollar Volume Percentages

	1	2	3	4
Item	**Unit Cost**	**Annual Usage (units)**	**Annual Usage (dollars)**	**% of Total Dollar Usage**
1	$4.00	1,250		
2	2.50	1,500		
3	3.00	10,000		
4	36.00	4,000		
5	31.00	12,500		
6	.517	8,000		
7	25.00	1,480		
8	325.00	100		
9	8.00	625		
10	6.00	1,000		
		Total		100%

2. Now, rank the answers from the highest annual usage to the lowest, and assign categories.

	1	2	3	4
Item	**Annual Usage (units)**	**% of Total**	**Cumulative %**	**Classification**

3. Define the following terms.

Physical Inventory Control:

Financial Inventory Control:

Cycle Counting:

Stock Keeping Unit (SKU):

ABC Classification:

4. Compare the push system and the pull system, as applied to production, material control and distribution.

Note to the Reader

In this book we've explored the competitive issues facing business today, and you've been introduced to the theory, tools and techniques that can make global manufacturing possible. We've discussed the long-term, medium-term and short-term planning processes, as well as how to evolve toward just-in-time manufacturing, and you've had an opportunity to practice using many tools. At this point you have the basic knowledge and skills necessary to launch and/or support your own continual improvement process. Now, what can you do each day to increase your net worth and make yourself more marketable in the manufacturing arena?

As the future unfolds in front of us and we bring new products to market faster and faster, I'm convinced that the manufacturing formula presented in this book will play a major role. But the most important role will be played by the portion of the formula that focuses on improving the forecasting process and the subsequent reduction in the forecast error. It is my hope that you will use this formula and the other tools successfully on the job, that you will teach others, and that as a result we will reach the critical mass required to manufacture on a global basis.

Good Luck.

Answers to Exercises

Module 2 Answers

1. Definitions:

   Business plan: a statement of long-range strategy supported by projection of resources.

   Manufacturing strategy: a strategy for the manufacturing function that includes assumptions required to support the long-term sales portion of the business plan.

   Production planning: an iterative process that results in three sets of figures: Year 1 projected sales, changes in inventory levels, and production levels.

   Production plan: a plan that results in projected production by year over the life of the business plan.

   Resource plan: a plan that determines the amount of resources (capacity) available.

2. Your answers could have included any of the following:

   - Mission statement
   - Objectives
   - Customers
   - Products and services
   - Competition
   - Current economic environment
   - Distribution channels
   - Production/sales and operation plan
   - Financial analysis
   - Major processes
   - Continuous process improvement
   - Functional strategies
   - Training and education strategy
   - Potential problems
   - Recommendations and implementation action plan

MODULE 2 ANSWERS (continued)

3. The basic manufacturing formula:

   Beginning inventory

   \+ *Production*

   = *Available inventory to ship (products to sell)*

   – *Shipments/sales*

   = *Ending inventory*

4. Did your answer look like the following?

Basic Manufacturing Formula	**Period**			
	1	**2**	**3**	**4**
Beginning Inventory	200	0	1,500	4,400
+ Production Requirement	3,800	6,000	4,100	6,000
= Available Products to Sell	4,000	6,000	6,600	10,400
– Projected Sales	4,000	4,500	2,200	6,400
= Ending Inventory	0	1,500	4,400	4,000
Average Inventory	100	750	2,200	4,200

Note: Remember, you had to fill the back order in Period 2 from Period 3's available products to sell.

Module 3 Answers (pages 40–41)

1. Your finished table should look like this:

					1	2	3	4
Work Center Number	**Work Center Descrip.**	**Number of Machines**	**Machine Use**	**Efficiency**	**Work Center Capacity in Hrs per Day**	**Units per Hours**	**Units per Day**	**Units per 20-Day Month**
700	Dip Insertion	2	.90	.90	12.96	5	64.80	1296
750	Axiel Insertion	4	.90	.85	24.48	7	171.36	3427
400	Cut & Clinch	6	.85	1.10	44.88	5	224.4	4488
020	Wave Solder	1	.90	.90	6.48	5	32.4	648
500	Automated Test Equipment	3	.80	1.05	20.16	6	120.9	2419
550	Functional Test	2	.90	1.00	14.4	4	57.6	1152

2. According to the data, the bottleneck work centers would appear to be: *020* and *550.*

3. Suggestions for increasing capacity:

Long-Term

- Add capital equipment
- Add facilities
- Develop long-term supplier relationships
- Use new technologies

MODULE 3 ANSWERS (continued)

Medium-Term

- Improve machine use and efficiency
- Add shifts
- Subcontract
- Improve units per hour (UPH)
- Add people
- Continuously improve the process

Short-Term

- Add overtime hours
- Subcontract (if already approved)
- Continuously improve process

4. *Customer Orders* + *Forecasted Orders* = shipment levels for coming periods.

5. Forecasting helps the manufacturer to

- improve customer service
- increase productivity
- estimate inventory
- improve deliveries from suppliers

6. *Shifts per day* ×
machines or work stations ×
hours per shift ×
utilization ×
efficiency ×
= *rated capacity*

Module 4 Answers (pages 57–59)

1. Your answer should include the following:

a. Product F is independent demand.

b. Product F is an end item/product.

c. Product F is part of the MPS.

d. Product F is forecasted.

e. Product F is a parent.

f. Product F is part of the BOM.

2. This is the information you should know about everything else below product F:

a. There are POs for items 1, 2, 3, 4, 5, 7, 8, 10, 11.

b. There are MOs for items F, G, B, J, N, Q, R and T.

c. Everything under product F is a component, raw material.

d. Everything under product F is dependent demand.

e. Everything under product F is part of MRP.

f. Everything under product F is calculated.

g. There are a number of parent component relationships.

h. It's a six-level BOM.

i. Alphabetical part numbers indicate manufactured items.

j. Numerical part numbers indicate purchased items.

MODULE 4 ANSWERS (continued)

3. Your completed chart should have the following answers.

Lead-time: **3 weeks** Lot size: **250**

Planning period = 9 periods

	Period								
	1	**2**	**3**	**4**	**5**	**6**	**7**	**8**	**9**
Gross Requirements	150	100	200	50	150	250	100	150	200
Scheduled Receipts	250								
Projected On Hand = 250	350	250	50	0	100	100	0	100	150
Net Requirements					–150	–150		–150	–100
Planned Order Receipts					250	250		250	250
Planned Order Release		250	250		250	250			

4. Fill-in-the-blank answers:

a. Material requirements planning

b. Independent demand

c. Dependent demand

d. Gross requirements

e. Planned order receipts

f. Planned order release

g. Net requirement

5. The reason for establishing a parent/component relationship is:

The parent/component relationship is first created when a new bill of material is entered into the system. It is primarily used to support the MRP gross-to-net logic from one level in the bill of material to the next.

Module 5 Answers (pages 73–74)

1. T
2. F (back scheduling)
3. F (build-to-stock)
4. F (finite loading)
5. T
6. F (input/output control)
7. T
8. T
9. T
10. F (infinite loading)
11. T
12. T
13. T
14. F (work center)
15. T

Module 6 Answers (pages 88–89)

1. The following are examples of waste in the traditional production environment:

- Excess inventory
- Cost incurred in carrying inventory
- Misuse of space
- Cost incurred such as rent and insurance expense
- Excessive material handling
- Use of machine capacity before needed and the related depreciation expense
- Quality problems related to moving and storing the inventory, and the associated costs
- Releasing lot sizes to production in larger quantities than called for in the master production schedule
- Excess inventory on the production floor, making "housekeeping" and visibility difficult
- Excessive manufacturing lead-time (queue, setup, run, wait, move)
- Requirements for inspection

MODULE 6 ANSWERS (continued)

2. JIT goals are achieved by:

- Improving housekeeping
- Reducing inventories
- Eliminating quality rejects
- Reducing lot sizes
- Reducing lead time
- Improving maintenance
- Simplifying processes
- Involving all levels of the company

3. Good supplier characteristics include:

- Delivers on time and in the right quantity
- Supplies parts that require no incoming inspection
- Sets fair prices and terms
- Cooperates to solve problems

4. The definitions are:

a. Demand pull is a visual feedback control system driven by customer demand.

b. The backflush is the updating—preferably monthly—of the accounting process and reconciling with the physical movement of parts, subassemblies and end items.

c. A count point is control point whenever in the manufacturing process counts are taken of parts, subassemblies and/or end products.

d. A production card indicates the quantity and part number to be produced, the materials and their location, etc.

e. A move card indicates the number of parts or subassemblies, etc., that are to move from one point in the production process to the next.

Module 7 Answers (pages 100–101)

1. Your completed chart should have the following information:

ABC Analysis Based on Annual Dollar Volume

A. Annual Dollar Volume Percentages

	1	2	3	4
Item	**Unit Cost**	**Annual Usage (units)**	**Anual Usage (dollars)**	**% of Total Dollar Usage**
1	$4.00	1,250	$5,000	.8
2	2.50	1,500	3,750	.6
3	3.00	10,000	30,000	4.6
4	36.00	4,000	144,000	22.0
5	31.00	12,500	387,500	59.0
6	.517	8,000	4,136	.6
7	25.00	1,480	37,000	5.6
8	325.00	100	32,500	5.0
9	8.00	625	5,000	.8
10	6.00	1,000	6,000	1.0
		Total	654,886	100%

MODULE 7 ANSWERS (continued)

2. The answers from the highest annual usage (dollars) to the lowest, and their ABC category.

	1	2	3	4
Item	Annual Usage (units)	% of Total	Cumulative %	Classification
5	387,500	59.0	59.0	A
4	144,000	22.0	81.0	A
7	37,000	5.6	86.6	B
8	32,500	5.0	91.6	B
3	30,000	4.6	96.2	B
10	6,000	1.0	97.2	C
1	5,000	.8	98.0	C
9	5,000	.8	98.8	C
6	4,136	.6	99.4	C
2	3,750	.6	100.0	C

3. Definitions:

   Physical Inventory Control: The determination of inventory quantity by actual count.

   Financial Inventory Control: The reconciliation of physical inventory on hand to accounting records.

   Cycle Counting: The counting of a certain number of items every workday with each item counted at a prescribed frequency.

   Stock Keeping Unit (SKU): An item located at a particular geographic location.

   ABC Classification: A cycle counting system used to determine the frequency of counting parts based on the value of usage.

4. *Push System:* Pushes inventory from a centered factory out into the warehouse. In distribution, replenishment decisions are centralized.

   Pull system: Pulls inventory from finished goods and delivers to the customer. In distribution, replenishment decisions are made at the field warehouse itself using an order point system.

NOTES

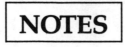

OVER 150 BOOKS AND 35 VIDEOS AVAILABLE IN THE 50-MINUTE SERIES